OLD FORT ST. VRAIN

Presented by:
Platteville Historical Society
PO Box 567
Platteville, CO 80651

OLD FORT ST. VRAIN

By

Diane Brotemarkle

Northern Plains Public Library
Ault Colorado

Cover art by Don Borie, Platteville, Colorado. Old Fort St. Vrain (looking east). The original watercolor has been donated to the Platteville Pioneer Museum. Printed by Johnson Books, Boulder, Colorado and published in association with the Platteville Historical Society.

Inside front cover: "Historic Trails Map: The Greeley Quadrangle" by Glenn R. Scott. Courtesy U.S. Geological Survey.

Library of Congress Cataloging-in-Publication Data
(LCCN) 2001118776

ISBN 0-9712372-0-4

Printed in the United States by
Johnson Printing
1880 South 57th Court
Boulder, Colorado 80301

Table of Contents

Acknowledgements

I wish to thank the following friends and acquaintances for their help and support over the last two years during which this manuscript was being developed: Joyce Carr and Bonnie Smith and the members of the Centennial Chapter of the DAR. in Greeley, staff at the Greeley Municipal Museum for sharing facsimiles of the St. Vrain Record Book, Susan Hoskinson, Director at Fort Vasquez, Platteville, for books ideas, and friendship. Leon Burlieu, voyageur, his wife Molly, and our *adobero* at Fort Vasquez, Mateos Alvarez; and Joe Pinner and his employer, the Fort St. Vrain Power Plant for including us and the old fort on their web site. Zethyl Gates of Loveland, for sharing her collection and her writings as well as her perspective on this area during the fur trade era. Mrs. Bessie St. Vrain her daughter and granddaughter for the St. Vrain family history. I am grateful to Darrell and Sandy Schulte who kept an eye out for good research materials on their travels and enhanced my reference library accordingly. I also want to thank Greg Holt, Director of Interpretation at Old Bent's Fort, National Park Service site, for his generosity in allowing me access to the library and archives. In a similar way, I owe a debt of gratitude to Sandra Lowry, archivist and librarian at Fort Laramie, National Park Service site and to the Curry family of Scottsbluff, Nebraska and Wheatland, Wyoming for introducing me to researchers there. Many hours of research at the Denver Public library's Western History Department were facilitated by its wonderful staff, especially volunteer Glenn R. Scott, formerly with the U.S. Geographic Survey, Phil and many others. The staff at the National Archives in Denver were most helpful toward research about the Upper Platte and Arkansas Indian Agency. Weld County historian Carol Shwayder shared her rich knowledge without stint, as well as her extensive library on the fur trade and Colorado history. Finally, I cannot thank enough the members of the Platteville Historical Society for their encouragement and support. Susan Hoskinson and Sally Miller critiqued portions of the manuscript.

Foreword

The St. Vrain name is prevalent in the locale between Longmont and Platteville, Colorado, from western Boulder County to South Central Weld County. There is a St. Vrain Creek or River, a St. Vrain valley, a St. Vrain school and school district. Many commercial enterprises use the famous name. Three miles northwest of Platteville the power generating plant, Fort St. Vrain, is once again active, though not now nuclear powered. Two or three miles more along the South Platte River one finds the site of the first Fort St. Vrain, named for the merchant who, together with Charles and then William Bent, had established the Bent, St. Vrain Trading Company in the 1830's: successful fur trade businesses at Taos, Bent's Fort, and, at last, Fort St. Vrain. His name was Ceran St. Vrain and of his influence and distinguished family more will be said later.

Old Fort St. Vrain, then, was located about six miles northwest of present Platteville, Colorado. As the major outpost of Bent's Fort in the 1840's and the largest of the four forts along the South Platte River, it had a prestigious pedigree among trading forts of the western American frontier. As merely one of "the four forts," however, it has never found its own niche on the history bookshelves of our libraries.

When it was suggested to me as an appropriate topic for a book (since it is a local landmark and close by my home), I worried about venturing into "history" since I am trained as a writer, folklorist, and literary critic. I kept hearing the voice of Sergeant Friday echoing through the decades: "Just the facts, ma'am." I hoped that by complying, I would avoid pitfalls created by my lack of expertise in historical analysis or the examination of the causes of events.

i

In the process of writing, however, I found the "facts" constantly misbehaving—contradicting one another, arranging themselves into narratives of dubious authenticity. I also found that I had overestimated my control over the book's content. Entire chapters seemed to insist on rearranging themselves into a different order which suggested quite different meanings than those I had assigned. I found myself in the discomfitting position, halfway through the writing, of not understanding my own creation and having great difficulty explaining to others what precisely I was doing about Old Fort St. Vrain.

Then, too, there were the stories. One cannot write about the west of the 1840's without discovering accounts by travelers and frontiersmen which are laced with a lot of spun yarn. My background, however, often led me to feel much more comfortable with the folk tales than with the facts. To my surprise, I was back in the arena of my own "expertise"! The scholarly challenge now became not only the maintaining of distinctions between verified or greatly coherent accounts which we deem "historical," and obvious fictions, but also that of creating explanations to show how the stories functioned in the unsettled cultures of America's nineteenth century frontier, at least in the valleys of the South Platte River. This is how the book evolved, as much a product of discovery as of creation, of coming to understand how the material might best be presented.

The approach is scholarly in the sense that research is documented and sources credited. In-text parenthetical references are intended to refer the reader to the "Works Consulted" section for full disclosure of publication data as in the MLA style used for humanities books. End of chapter notes expand upon or qualify textual material, occasionally including source references. Documentation should be correct and instructive but not intrusive to the reader, and so I have tried to be as honest and charitable to my sources as is fair without becoming overly intrusive on the reader's concentration upon a text.

There has been only one publication devoted exclusively to Old Fort St. Vrain. In October of 1952, LeRoy Hafen, then the Colorado State Historian, published his summary about the site but this was a brief treatment and appeared in the Colorado Historical Society's magazine called *Colorado Magazine*. Although the traders and trappers of the 1840's receive the bulk of attention, Hafen also mentions the fact that Old Fort St. Vrain was the first county seat of Weld County, created simultaneously with Colorado Territory in 1861. Finally, preservation issues loomed greatly in Hafen's mind, since the integrity of the site was at risk from ranching activities nearby. These three topics, then, suggested an outline: Fort St. Vrain experienced a fur trade era, and secondly a period of private settlement and governmental focus. Thirdly, it remained a concern for preservation-minded Coloradans, so that, from time to time, it was recalled in newspaper accounts of the earliest Colorado history. This outline became the basis for a brief essay I wrote for the Platteville Historical Society's Archaeology and Preservation Week observances in 1998. It remains the skeleton for this extended treatment which has resulted both from a desire to correct some errors and misleading statements in my brochure as well as to synthesize scattered references about the trading post and to add some new information.

Accordingly, then, I begin with the earliest days of Fort St. Vrain, rendering biographical information about the persons who were there for the purposes of the fur trade, beaver and bison. The Hispanic-style architecture and the making of adobe bricks tell the story of the material culture of the South Platte trading posts. The second chapter relates a story about Old Fort St. Vrain written by a long-time resident of this area, Marshall Cook. Here, and in two subsequent chapters, any information that bears on the question of its authenticity is presented in "argument" and often with other stories from early sojourners in the Rocky Mountain West. A major thesis thus emerged, the question whether Cook's account of the massacre of the Arapaho Indians at Fort St. Vrain was history or folk tale, and if it is a little bit of both, to clarify which is which. The third chapter is about Fort St. Vrain's manager, Marcellin St. Vrain, his family and heritage. What clues are there in Marcellin's biography that help lend credibility to Cook's account? The offering of evidence about the credibility of Cook's account continues in the fourth chapter with a study of John Fremont's character and the great influence of Fremont's expedition with the Topographical Engineers on the subsequent history of the fort—and how a fourth of July was celebrated at Fort. St. Vrain with the strange circumstances of its aftermath. The following chapters focus on Old Fort St. Vrain itself. I present some little-known information about Fort St. Vrain as an Indian Agency, part of the Upper Platte and Arkansas Agency. The three agents who parleyed at Fort St. Vrain most often—Thomas Fitzpatrick, John Whitfield, and Thomas Twiss—all had interesting problems and lives. In Chapter Six, the uses of Fort St. Vrain during the Colorado gold rush are explained, with the members and activities of the St. Vrain Claim Club. Chapter Seven, called "Dedication," uses the term as a double entendre, referring to the work of the Daughters of the American Revolution and the Colorado Sons of the Revolution, as well as many early Colorado pioneers, in preserving old trails and early forts; hence the dedication of the monument at Fort St. Vrain. As well, a few scattered agencies and individuals have been dedicated to creating and preserving the monument's site, so it is more accessible to visitors. Various land use issues have always created a set of problems. Ranching and mining interests continue to put pressure on the pristine setting of the site. Those kinds of questions will determine whether Old Fort St. Vrain has a future or not.

This, then, is not only a history book but is, in a way, a book about history. If it is unified, the interplay between folklore and history (with Marshall Cook's "early history" as a prime example) is the unifying thrust. But the site itself is the star of this show—as Marshall Cook said—"if 'doby walls could speak, what a story they would tell." This book is some portion of that story. The result will not satisfy all readers. Some may disagree with my judgments regarding fiction and fact. Some may reject my interpretations of either or dislike interpretation, editorializing and theorizing. The best I could do was compromise and leave some of the theorizing to the notes which interested readers may study and those not interested may ignore. Much of the honesty of a book like this is in recognizing and accepting controversy as healthy. I hope this book is never boring and that it stimulates readers to join me in a dialogue about the ways history and folklore may cooperate in bringing us to better understand ourselves and the culture that shapes so much of our individual destinies. For in the final analysis, we want the books we read to educate us about "their stories" and bring us to meditate on the possibilities for them to become and to be "our stories."

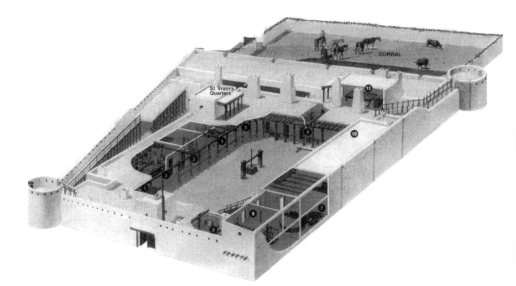

Lower level
1. Council Room
2. Trade Room
3. Dining Room
4. Cook's Room
5. Kitchen
6. Blacksmith & Carpenter Quarters
7. Warehouses
8. Laborer's Quarters

Old Fort St. Vrain was a smaller version of Bent's Old Fort, pictured here. The lower level, though not the upper levels, provides an architectural model. Courtesy National Park Service.

I. Bent's Fort of the South Platte

It all began—if there is such a thing as a beginning–in the early fall of 1836 when William Bent rode on horseback with a few companions along the Old Trappers' Trail, the east bank (often) of the South Platte River, which meandered down from the Middle Park of the central Rockies, before a Colorado was ever dreamed of and when this land was Indian land, or, perhaps the "Unorganized Territory" of the Louisiana Purchase. The trail known as Trappers' Trail was overlayed by another, the Taos Trail, used by the Taos traders by way of Bent's Fort on the Arkansas as they traveled north to Fort St. Vrain and Fort Laramie.

The river flows northeast until it joins the North Platte in southwestern Nebraska, not far off the Oregon Trail. Bent, whom the Indians called "Little White Man," was the proprietor of Bent's Fort, 250 miles southeast, situated along the "mountain branch" of the Santa Fe Trail, a frequent stopover for those travelling the Taos Trail. For several years he and his partners, his brother Charles Bent and Ceran St. Vrain, had hoped to build a major outpost to the north of Bent's Fort close by the Northern Cheyenne and Sioux hunting grounds. In 1833, this dream had been thwarted when the trading company of Robert Campbell and William Sublette, the Rocky Mountain Fur Company, had built Fort William, now known as Fort Laramie, to the north, in the center of the Sioux Indian hunting and trading grounds. Then, by 1835, Sublette's younger brother Andrew had entered into a partnership with Louis Vasquez to establish an adobe trading post about halfway between Fort Laramie and Bent's Fort, in the lands of

1

the Arapaho and Northern Cheyenne Indians. The wagon traders, hired by the Bent, St. Vrain Co. to haul wares to temporary camps along the creeks, had reported yet another adobe trading post, nine miles south of Fort Vasquez—the dream of one Lancaster P. Lupton.

Bent's survey of the situation soon confirmed that even a third semi-permanent trading post had been established in this neighborhood—Fort Jackson, the only one (according to some theorists) on the west bank of the South Platte, about halfway between Fort Lupton and Fort Vasquez. It was run by Peter Sarpy and Henry Fraeb of the American Fur Company. Its architecture and precise location are not known and so rumors persist that it was the only South Platte trading post on the west side of the river; it may have been a wooden stockade structure rather than adobe. All three commercial ventures (none were ever military forts) were within ten miles of one another! Clearly the competition was already too heated for an undercapitalized trading post to survive. But Bent, St. Vrain Co. was not undercapitalized and these rivals were drawing the Arapaho, Northern Cheyenne, and perhaps other Indian trade away from Bent's Fort with these convenience-store establishments.[1] Bent's hopes for the Sioux trade had been severely damaged with Campbell and Sublette's Fort William on the Laramie. Now it was imperative that the company answer these challenges. They applied to William Clark in St. Louis and the trading license for the fourth of the South Platte trading posts was issued November 8, 1836 to the Bent, St. Vrain Co. It would construct a major company outpost just seven miles north of Fort Vasquez on the South Platte—to be named Fort Lookout.

The word went out from Bent's Fort, across the Arkansas River, to Mexico, on the opposite bank. *Adoberos* were being hired to build yet another adobe structure, and William Bent's younger brother George with the Mexican adobe workers was sent to the South Platte location in the spring and summer of 1837, to oversee the construction project. From that year until the company closed down the trading post temporarily in 1846 or 47, it was known in company circles and communications

2

not as Fort Lookout but as Fort George. When the post was completed in 1837, and opened the next summer for business, the youngest of the St. Vrains, Marcellin, brother of Ceran, was installed as proprietor and "booshway." Whether George Bent had hoped for the appointment is not known. Perhaps senior partner Charles Bent—whom the prolific author David Lavender said was always the mediator in company business[2] —had negotiated some controversy or other and the young Marcellin St. Vrain won the post. Perhaps George Bent did not want the post. In any event, the mountain men, hunters, travelers and traders, called the adobe trading post, "St. Vrain's" and that, despite official records of government or company, was the name that stuck.

George Bent carried with him the instructions for the architecture at Bent's Fort, modeled on the Hispanic hacienda style buildings that the company partners had seen in Taos and Santa Fe. Fort St. Vrain was made of bricks, dried in the summer sun and composed of sandy clay soil, found readily along the South Platte, and of the natural hay which grew abundantly and provided the grass roots binder for the adobe structure. Adobe had the advantage of providing cool rooms in summer and warmth in winter. It was nearly fireproof, an excellent defense against hostile attack.

Old Fort St. Vrain was 127' by 106' and featured inner walls whose roofs were supported by wood poles, for rooms on two sides. These mud, gravel and thatch-roofed partitions provided guest lodgings, permanent residents' quarters (for the manager and family), trade and council rooms, storage for furs and buffalo robes in compressed bundles, hired hands' sleeping and mess quarters, and an annex (probably on the east side of Fort St. Vrain) for the quality livestock to be corralled and protected against theft. Two round towers on the northeast and southwest corners allowed for watchmen to defend the fort against the approach of hostiles. Perhaps, like Bent's Fort, Fort St. Vrain's nearly fourteen foot high walls were lined with prickly pear cactus plants to discourage intruders.

The entrance—double doors wide enough for wagons to come and go from the courtyard—faced south and slightly eastward. There was a smaller Dutch door, used to exchange goods if the company personnel did not want to admit customers into the fort's interior. A massive fireplace large enough for a blacksmith to repair equipment, wagons, shoe horses and mules, was set along a north wall and perhaps had a counterpart outside the walls. In a corner the well—probably lined with lime—supplied drinking water.

One sometimes reads accounts by travelers who called these buildings, "sod houses." An adobe structure is not technically the same as a sod house, even though the two terms were alternately used in early travelers' letters and journals. The nomenclature of the time may have justified this. Today, however, it is useful to think in terms of their differences. Adobe-making is a more complex process which involves mixing sand, clay soil, straw or grass roots, and water. The recipe calls for these ingredients in about a 40-40-10-10 ratio. This thick batter is poured into wooden gang-molds about 2 by 12 by 24 inches. When the brick is sufficiently dry to hold its

Fort St. Vrain's deteriorating walls are shown in Francis Cragin's photos taken November, 1903. The camera faces east. The prairie has since been leveled. Colorado Springs Pioneer Museum. Used with permission.

shape, it is turned out of its mold and dries or "bakes" in the summer sun. After about six weeks, a brick will have cured. The walls are then created by stacking cured bricks in a herringbone pattern, sometimes with pebbles for mortar if fine enough gravel is available, or with rougher adobe fragments. According to one observer, Fort St. Vrain did not have this fill between bricks. The adobe mud is also made into a thinner slip coat or plaster, which is smoothed over the bricks.

On the other hand, the sod houses built by pioneers could be constructed in a day. A sod house was intended as temporary shelter until a sturdier structure could be erected. The settler sought a "buckskin spot," a barren section where the ground was so tough that nothing would grow, but this packed earth made a decent floor for a prairie home. Within the buckskin spot, a square space would be marked out, ideally at least sixteen by twenty feet, for a two-room house. In a later decade, after the American Civil War, the Homestead legislation advised or required certain dimensions. The prairie soil where the grass was thickest was then broken up, most efficiently by a team of oxen pulling a plow, the blade of which was set for four inch cuts. Once the sod was "busted" in this way, pioneers used spades and shovels to cut the sod into strips twenty-eight inches long. The sod pieces were loaded onto a crude sled and drawn by horse, mule, or oxen team, manpower if necessary, to the building site. A row of sod blocks was laid around the staked rectangle. Again, the herringbone pattern, which does not allow vertical and horizontal joints to meet, makes a strong, quite stable structure. Thus, in the final stages, modern brick homes, adobe, and sod construction processes are much alike. But the pioneering owners of the sod house, relieved as they might be to have any kind of shelter away from covered wagons and canvas tents, would quickly begin to plan for a proper dwelling made of lumber and shingled roofs. Of course, the old sod houses often served prairie families as living quarters for employees or relatives for many years after they were built.[3]

True to the hacienda style architecture, the adobe fort or trading post features uncovered space in the center, a courtyard or *placita,* open to the sun and stars, for welcoming guests, for holding fiestas, fandangos, and sometimes Indian ceremonial dances. And two round towers, on the northeast and southwest corners, had been built two stories high at Fort St. Vrain, containing an upper loft with a loophole, sometimes called a "gunwale" in each one, together with a fireplace by which the watchman might keep warm in winter. The outer walls would also be interspersed with loopholes, so called, according to General O.O. Howard in his memoir for children called *Indian Chiefs I Have Known,* because the grass used as adobe binder was let drop to provide a shade for the square opening and then, when necessary, looped up over the top of the wall for sighting beyond with spyglass or firearms.

During its eight year existence as an Indian trading post, Fort St. Vrain had the advantage of being recommended to those northbound travelers who stopped at the parent enterprise, Bent's Fort. Thus, all types of visitors must sometimes have crossed through its double doors, for like Bent's Fort, Fort St. Vrain provided a focus for such social and communal gatherings as were possible for restless American nomads, expansionists, trappers, traders, pioneers, wayfarers, missionaries, doctors, adventurers both white and indigenous. Many left commentaries about it in journal entries, letters, travelogues. It was, in its time, an important transportation link, safely along waterways, on a north-south axis between the Santa Fe trail to the south and the Oregon Trail to the north. The road past it, the Trapper/Taos/Cherokee trails as it was variously known by persons with a variety of interests for traveling that route, followed the South Platte, varying somewhat from season to season as flood or drought dictated.[4]

George Bent Jr.,the son of William Bent and his Cheyenne wife, Owl Woman—the nephew of William's brother George Bent who oversaw construction at Fort St. Vrain—corroborated the existence of the outpost while reminiscing about Bent's Fort and placed it squarely in a company context:

> . . . in later years two branch forts were established by the Bent and St. Vrain Company: Fort St. Vrain on the

Platte, opposite the mouth of St. Vrain's Fork, for the Sioux, Cheyenne and Arapaho trade, and Adobe Fort on the Canadian for the Kiowa, Comanche and Apache trade. These two forts, like Bent's Fort, were built of adobe. The St. Vrains usually had charge of Fort St. Vrain while my father was in command of Bent's Fort and Adobe. Bent's Fort was the company's headquarters. Besides these three main posts, the company established stockades and trading houses from time to time at different points in the plains, but these were usually abandoned after a few seasons. In the '40's, the Bent and St. Vrain Company was doing a larger business than any other American company with the exception of Astor's great fur company.[5]

Meanwhile, the commercial rivalries among the South Platte trading posts intensified, and this theme would pervade historical commentary for another century, as one finds in Seletha Brown's book about the four forts along the South Platte: *Rivalry Along the River,* a book which found inspiration from LeRoy Hafen's summary essay on Fort St. Vrain as well as earlier sources. Hafen's 1952 essay, described in the "Foreword," discussed Fort St. Vrain as one of four trading posts embroiled in competition for the Indian trade. One of the assumptions of the present book is that there is *more* to the story of Fort St. Vrain than this contest—but, as a summary of its fur trade era, the South Platte commercial rivalry deserves a brief review.

Fort Vasquez, constructed and managed by Louis Vasquez and Andrew Sublette was begun and apparently in operation in 1835. Shortly thereafter, Lancaster Platt Lupton, who had come with Colonel Dodge's dragoons in 1835, and who had resigned his army commission (he was a West Point graduate) built Fort Lancaster, popularly called Lupton's Fort. Third, Peter A. Sarpy and Henry Fraeb, seasoned mountain men like Vasquez and the Sublettes, built Fort Jackson perhaps on the west bank of the South Platte. By late 1836, when Bent, St. Vrain Company obtained their license for the Indian trade on the South Platte, these three establishments were underway. The Bent, St. Vrain Co. had had previously some presence in the valley. Clear evidence of this is found in the journal of Robert Newell, reporting events of the spring of 1836:

> In may I left the South Fork Platte, returned to the Arkansas fort. Settled with Bent & St. Vrain returned to the Platte with animals, delivered up my winters trade, made preparation to leave the mountains. In a few days all was ready. We left Sublette & Vasquez fort on the 19th of may. Our party now consists of three P[hillip] Thompson, myself, and a man we engaged to assist us in packing our little baggage. Sublette & Vasquez fort is about 12 miles [sic] from the mountains near Long's Peak.[6]

But substantial posts like that of Fort Vasquez and Fort Jackson had many advantages over the wagon and lean-to operation of a company trader like Newell. He would look forward to better quarters when the company built its own post there where the St. Vrain Creek meets the South Platte. Thus Fort Lookout on the South Platte came to be. There were several "Fort Lookout's" in the west of those days, but William Bent indulged in the repetition, one supposes, for he meant to keep an eye on business competition, not least of all because of possible or probable abuses of the laws prohibiting the exchange of alcohol in the Indian trade.

The Bent, St. Vrain Co.'s choice of location was not entirely dictated by proximity to the three posts already located on the South Platte. Rather, the location it chose reflected the options and concerns that had already been presented to the other three. The availability of clay soil was certainly a factor, for not all soil is appropriate for making adobe bricks. Thus, the availability of clay soil in that particular area provided a practical reason for locating permanent posts there. Secondly, the Rocky Mountain Fur Company (later merged into the American Fur Company) had essentially divided the Cheyenne Indians into northern and southern groups, the southern congregating around Bent's Fort, the northern drawn to Fort Laramie. Opening a post with the permanence and reliability of Bent's Fort halfway toward Fort Laramie would bring the whole Cheyenne tribe, hopefully, back into the Bent, St. Vrain clientele. Fort St. Vrain would draw the Northern Cheyenne business, at least in theory—and William Bent's close association with the tribe into which he had married certainly helped the company to attract both groups through familial loyalties. Thirdly, Marcellin St. Vrain's marriage to the Sioux child-woman Spotted Fawn was a typical ploy to attract her relatives southward from Fort Laramie. There is, too, a fourth reason, one which requires somewhat more explanation.

Bent, St. Vrain Co. wagons could be sent out to compete with the annual spring Rendezvous, the major gathering in early July established by William Ashley in the early 1830's, primarily to supply mountain men, especially the trappers of the American Fur Company, for the fall trapping season and to procure the beaver pelts and other hides the mountain men—both employees of the big companies and independent trappers—had amassed. By the mid 1830's this system had become grossly unfair. These temporary marketplaces near the central Rockies held monopolies; the eastern-based suppliers with their wagon trains, charged outrageously high prices for the coffee, sugar, traps, firearms, rum, and other goods that mountain men would need for the coming year. On their return to St. Louis or other Stateside cities, the middle men such as Pratte and Chouteau sold the furs at greatly inflated prices and the profits were enormous. Naturally, the trappers began to seek other means of disposing of their furry wares. We learn, for example, that Kit Carson was not present at the rendezvous at Horse Creek near Green River Wyoming in 1840. Instead, Carson and Jack Robinson went to Robidoux's fort in Utah country "and there disposed of the furs we had caught."[7] We find a second example in Robert Newell's journal, stating that on February 7, 1840, he left Brown's Hole with 300 beaver pelts and traveled to Fort Hall to obtain supplies and sell his furs.

Traders at Fort Crockett (in present northwestern Colorado) and Fort Robidoux "were obtaining supplies from the forts on the South Platte, while Fort Hall was being supplied by Hudson's Bay Company from Vancouver (Gowan 197). Not only could the trappers seek an outpost like Fort St. Vrain along the Front Range, but the company wagons could seek them out at camps along the creeks. Thus, the Bent, St. Vrain Company provided a place for trappers to gather in the early 1840's—and also served as a resupply station for its own wagons which would fan out along the creeks to serve mountain men's camps.

From the first, then, the competition was intense. During early September of 1839, a German, Dr. Frederick A. Wislizenus, passed by Fort St. Vrain on his way home from the mountain men's annual rendezvous along the Green River in present Wyoming. The doctor wrote:

> On September 3rd we were unexpectedly to the left [west] bank of the South Fork [Platte] and crossed. On the right bank here there are three forts only a few miles apart. These are Penn's and Savory's [Bent and St. Vrain's] Fort, Vasquez and Sublette's Fort and Lupton's Fort. They are of the customary construction, the outer walls being of 'doby. There is much enmity and jealousy between these places . . .[8]

Ever after this written record was translated from the German into English and printed in early Colorado histories, (e.g. Wilbur Stone's, 1916) the "competition among the four forts of the South Platte" made a handy unifying theme. Although being grouped with three other establishments in this way tended ultimately to obscure Fort St. Vrain's history, it competed and in a sense "won" the competition. In 1838 the Bent, St. Vrain Company absorbed the entirety of Fort Jackson's inventory. Then there were three forts on the South Platte. By 1842 Fort Vasquez, having changed ownership to no avail, was closed down as a trading post for the last time. Lancaster Lupton moved his business from the South Platte to a location adjacent to Fort Laramie in 1844. According to David Lavender, in his book about the Bent, St. Vrain Co., its tactics had been aggressive and deliberate. In a fortunately preserved letter from one trader (not related to the South Platte competition) to his business associate and brother, we obtain a sense of the import of Dr. Wizlizenus' comment and realize that the intense vying for hides was endemic in the fur trade all through its history, with all companies keeping a lookout on rivals from the huge Hudson Bay Co. or the American Fur Co. of John Jacob Astor to the smallest crew of independent trappers. It can therefore be misleading to overstate rivalries in the immediate vicinity of the South Platte, whose trade wars were, relatively speaking, a tempest in a teapot of commercial competitions from Canada to Mexico.

By January of 1839, when Marcellin St. Vrain had been Fort St. Vrain's manager for about a year, the twenty-three year old was, says Lavender, "going hog wild."

> He [Marcellin St. Vrain] was a slight youth, about five and a half feet tall and only 115 pounds or so in weight. He loved whiskey, horse racing and hunting. . . . Made open-handed by liberal portions of his own trade alcohol, he was now offering one he-mule or one horse for ten [buffalo] robes. Outrageous prices— but the Picotte brothers, trading for the [rival] American Fur Company's Sioux Outfit and feeling the effect of Marcellin's prodigality, admitted he was raking in business. 'We are obliged,' Joe Picotte wrote his brother Honore, 'to let go the hand [that is, be equally generous] if we want to have a few hides'[9].

As St. Vrain's neighboring trading posts folded, their employees drifted to other concerns. Bent, St. Vrain Co. had been paying wages somewhat above the going rate, also, in order to entice competitors' labor force into their own. In this way, for example, James Beckwourth, the controversial, legendary, and much discussed mulatto mountain man, left Vasquez and then Lancaster Lupton and went to work for

11

Marcellin St. Vrain, probably as a hunter to supply the fort with meat. Jean Baptiste Charbonneau, "Bap," the son of Sacajawea and the French voyageur, Toussaint, who had made Lewis and Clark's epic journey across the West as an infant tied to his mother's back, was among the traders who carried Bent, St. Vrain trade goods to Indian clients downstream from Fort St. Vrain along the South Platte River.

As needed, Bent's Fort on the Arkansas sent willing employees from the Arkansas River on missions to their South Platte outpost. Many of these hands remain part of the recorded history of earliest Colorado Euro-American activity, and the list includes: Alex Godey. For bravery and integrity he might have been as famous as his friend Kit Carson. Godey was for several years employed as a hunter at Fort St. Vrain and eventually achieved limited fame as one of John Fremont's indispensable guides and guards. Godey earned the usual wages for humility and has been almost forgotten. When Fremont, who hired Godey away from Fort St. Vrain in 1843, recalled the fort scene, he found Seth Ward the head trader. Seth Ward's son became the son-in-law of northeastern Colorado's first permanent resident, Elbridge Gerry. Ward was better remembered as the sutler of Fort Laramie; he eventually retired to a lavish estate in St. Louis. William Bransford, who was involved with General Kearny's invasion into Mexico in 1846, and who fell in love with Marcellin St. Vrain's young Indian wife, worked as a wagon trader using Fort St. Vrain as headquarters from 1844 to 1849. "Uncle Dick" Wootton, who built the first "two story" commercial store in Denver and who helped William Byers launch the *Rocky Mountain News* in 1859, rode a weekly route during the early 1840's on horseback between Bent's Fort and Fort St. Vrain, across the route called Smokey Hill. His memory of these many rides is summed up in his autobiography, a brief paragraph, where he recalls that he often carried large sums of gold and silver coin—and never lost so much as two bits for his employers.[10] From these dashes, John Fremont perhaps suggested the idea of a "pony express" mail route to his influential father-in-law, Senator Thomas Benton. Whether or not the claim is clearly justified, local historians and journalists have charged to the credit of Fort St. Vrain some responsibility for inaugurating the Pony Express.[11]

The list also includes John Simpson Smith, another cart trader out of Fort St. Vrain. One of the founding fathers of Denver in the late 1850's, he had become fluent in the Cheyenne and Arapaho languages by doing business along the South Platte. In later days, his interpreter skills were often required, since negotiations among Indian agents for the government, the white settlements and the Indian encampments (the land was, after all, until the early 1860's, legally the Indians')—these parleys were constantly bumped happenstance along from crisis to crisis. Names like Bill New, Mexican Sol Silver, and even more shadowy figures of trapper and mere transient, remind us that Fort St. Vrain in 1846 was a developmental cornerstone of what would become Colorado, the Centennial State, thirty years later. Two eventualities— municipal rivals Denver and Greeley taking center stage, and transportation corridors bypassing the old Fort—would eventually blur the role of Fort St. Vrain in the memories of many Colorado historians, but in the recollections of the first settlers and early pioneers the foundational role of the last of the adobe South Platte trading forts was not to be forgotten.

Many of these St Vrain employees, aware of their singular roles on the frontier, wrote autobiographies, and many achieved historical niches because they were the subject of explorer Fremont's praise or of academicians' biographies: James Beckwourth, Seth Ward, Kit Carson, Uncle Dick Wootton, Alex Godey, John Simpson Smith. Of these, the man who took honors among those named on the lapidary inscription on the DAR monument at Fort St. Vrain, perhaps the most renowned person of all the early employees of Bent, St. Vrain Co., was Kit Carson, Indian agent, Indian fighter— guide of the first two of Fremont's mapping expeditions.

Carson truly seems to have been the inspiration for the archetypal western hero—not only able but invincible, lucky, brave, resourceful, and humble—magnificently effective but ever self-effacing. American folklorists writing of the west have outlined this as a version of heroism, a fictional paradigm, played out eternally by the Lone Ranger—the self-effacing messiah, anonymous, successful, leaving his audience gasping happily, "Who was that masked man?" Reviewing the testimonials appended to the 1926 edition of Kit Carson's autobiography, one finds his acquaintances describing him with the following adjectives and phrases: "He was brave but never reckless . . . unselfish, a veritable exponent of Christian altruism; and as true to his friends as steel to the magnet (Inman, 1897); he impressed you at once as a man of rare kindliness and charity, such as a truly brave man ought always to be. As simple as a child but as brave as a lion, he took our hearts by storm and grew upon our regard all the while we were with him (James Rusling, quoting Gen. W.T. Sherman, 1857); quiet, modest, retiring . . . dignified . . . a gentleman . . . one of nature's noblemen—a true man in all that constitutes manhood—pure—honorable—truthful—sincere—of noble impulses, a true knight-errant ever ready to defend the weak against the strong, without reward other than his own conscience . . . Carson had great contempt for noisy braggarts and shame of every sort; bravery, high-toned honour, integrity and simplicity of character . . . the truest and best friend the red men of the West ever had, and yet in war he was their worst enemy . . . (H.R. Tilton, 1874).

Thus was Kit Carson deeply mourned. He was endowed with such an admirable balance between heroic skill and humility that he may seem realizable only in those "sentimental" memoirs called fictions. And yet, who are we to deny these eye-witnesses? Carson was known for devotion to his wife Josepha, and yet his lifestyle called him to be absent from her for many months at a stretch. She was of the type to cope with this; she pre-deceased him holding him ever in loving regard even as he mourned her passing as a harbinger to his own. One feels that we ought to affirm this version of the biography of a real westerner because we "need" heroes, or so we are told. But what we really need is truth. It seems that the name of Kit Carson inscribed on the DAR monument at Fort St. Vrain, little though it may now be noted, recalls that kind of need.

He is interesting to this writer because in him authentic folklore and historical truth intersect, the sort of dovetailing without which America would be culturally bankrupt.

One last point: Kit Carson was one of the "Taos traders," and came to Fort St. Vrain from a southern base along the Sante Fe Trail and the southwest. The geographical affinity of Fort St. Vrain to the people, towns and commercial establishments to the *south* is important to its history because when Bent's Fort on the Arkansas ceased to flourish, this northernmost extension of the Taos Trail became isolated from its own reason for being, and this would later contribute to the amnesia of historians regarding it. Nor could it recover an identity as Fort Laramie flourished along the Oregon Trail since the U.S. Army purchased Fort Laramie in 1849 and it became part of military history and somewhat detached from its commercial history. As for Fort St. Vrain, because it offered shelter, it was continually a stopover, but because it had no resident manager after 1850, it had no other amenities or hospitality. Its frequent commerce with Fort Laramie and its continued use on the north-south traffic of westward expansion meant that it had a fascinating history, but its story cannot not be told in full so long as our sense of history is dominated by traditional spatial or geographical orientations. Fort St. Vrain lost an important geographical identity when it was no longer used by the Taos traders.

After the last of the South Platte rival forts went out of business in 1844, Bent, St. Vrain Co. decided to close Fort St. Vrain during the summer, opening the fort for business only in winter months when the furs and bison robes were at their season's peak of lushness. Summer was always the slow season of the fur trade in any case, the season when the Bent, St. Vrain traders took their annual haul to St. Louis and purchased goods for the following trade season to bring back by wagon train, across the Santa Fe Trail to Taos, then to Santa Fe where the company's mercantile stores were resupplied, then to Bent's Fort and lastly to the outposts such as Fort St. Vrain. However, by the late spring of 1846, when General Stephen Watts Kearny's Army of the West was poised at Bent's Fort for its invasion into Mexico, (at that time Mexico was just across the Arkansas River) summer travelers found Fort St. Vrain supposedly "abandoned" and accounts of its closure began to circulate.

For example, in the summer of 1846 the journalist Francis Parkman found the site in what he considered bad repair and published in his book *The Oregon Trail* an account of its "desertion" which has been so often repeated, taught, read and reread that it creates a benediction upon the site which might have surprised William Bent and the other shareholders in the Bent, St. Vrain Trading Co. Parkman wrote: ". . . the walls of unbaked brick were cracked from top to bottom . . . the heavy gates torn from their hinges and flung down. The area within was overgrown with weeds, and the long ranges of apartments, once occupied by the motley concourse of traders, Canadians, and squaws, were miserably dilapidated."[12]

A year earlier, in 1845, William B. Franklin commented as he passed Fort St. Vrain and the other South Platte trading posts: "These are all deserted now, the trade having become too small to support them."[13] These two accounts by passersby seem to be offering identical testimony; in fact, both writers leaped to the same conclusion—that the fate of three competing forts was mutual self-destruction—although, unbeknownst to either, they were witnessing quite different phenomena. Forts Vasquez and Lupton had indeed closed down, but Fort St. Vrain's management was experiencing a series of crises that left the premises empty on occasion.

There is a distinct difference between "going out of business" as had occurred at Ft. Lupton and Fort Vasquez between 1842 and 1844 and "Gone on vacation," which was more like the situation for Fort St. Vrain management in 1845. By leaving the fort completely unmanned in the summer, the company guaranteed that the routine adobe upkeep—a task only doable in the hot summer months—would be left undone. Consequently, the walls would show each year's erosion from wind and rain and passers-by would notice its "derelict" condition.

The summer of 1846 was made even more confusing to western historians because just about all the fort employees

16

rushed to Bent's Fort to make themselves useful to General Stephen Watts Kearny for his renowned foray into Mexico. Marcellin St. Vrain did not post a sign at Fort St. Vrain saying "Off to war," but he went to Bent's Fort on the Arkansas to fill in as "booshway" while William Bent scouted for the Army.

The previous March of 1846 Marcellin presumably witnessed the birth of his daughter Mary Louise at Fort St. Vrain. His presence there at that time would be consistent with the revised "open-in-winter-only" schedule which the Bent, St. Vrain Co. had adopted after 1844 when Lupton left the South Platte country. By August, 1846, Marcellin was at the Arkansas River main post, Bent's Fort. He had had some "trouble with the Indians" around Fort St. Vrain. Thus, that summer, Marcellin St. Vrain became embroiled in his own personal problems, too, and these would result in his hospitalization near his St. Louis family's home estate. Loyal employees such as William Bransford would return to Fort St. Vrain.

The crises had in the meantime multiplied, particularly with the deaths of Willliam's wife Owl Woman and his two brothers, the older one, Charles who was massacred in the "Taos Uprising," of 1847 and the next, George. Between the St. Vrain brothers, tensions escalated when Marcellin St. Vrain returned to St. Louis and was reluctant to return to his South Platte post. Ceran St. Vrain, unable to cope with his grief and frustration, sold his share of the company and by 1849 William Bent found himself sole owner of the prestigious business. He had his own frustrations: the U.S. Army made use of Bent's Fort and might have purchased it had William Bent not been offended at the low price his government offered. Old Bent's Fort was blown up by Bent himself and William turned north to Fort St. Vrain for awhile before he returned to the Arkansas to build the New Bent's Fort.

According to David Lavender, who employs a little "poetic license," the northern plain Indians ". . . gravitated around the tributaries of the Platte. This, coupled to the proximity of the Oregon Trail, led William to repair temporarily Fort St. Vrain . . . Mexican labor was still cheap. Soon the motley concourse reoccupied the apartments, the Indians danced again

17

on the placita, and the benign Little White Man once more gratified them with presents . . ." As for the emigrant trade, the "Bent traders did not carry even their own groceries northward, They swapped food with the pilgrims, sold animals, purchased the caravan's worn-out oxen for a song, fattened the beasts up along the South Platte, and resold them at fancy markups to later trains" (Lavender 341-2). The latter practice was stock-in-trade (to take advantage of a pun) for all the major destinations of the emigrant hordes. Many of those at Fort Laramie who were pinched to buy "fresh" animals complained of the additional hardship on an incredibly hard journey, but in the last analysis those who could get draft animals anywhere along the route were among the more fortunate. The bottomlands along the South Platte north of Denver produced natural hay of the highest quality, ideal for raising and restoring livestock, and Old Fort St. Vrain must have witnessed the fall ritual of swathing it by hand and putting up the hay every season from 1840 onward. Thus in a strict literal sense, Fort St. Vrain was never absolutely "abandoned," but its use and neglect varied, as with all human creations.

As the Indians redeveloped and strengthened their own trade networks, the era of the mountain man and trapper came to an end. Many drifted back to Taos or onward to California—a few seeking adventure as far as Australia. However, many stayed on, providing continuity between the 1840's era of the trapper and trader and the rather different world along the South Platte of the 1850's.

Had William Bent foreseen, in 1836 during his excursion to the South Platte, that the market for beaver plews would crash within three years—or that the South Platte River would turn out to be unreliable for portage, or that his closest family members would die and the company be dissolved within the next dozen years—and his historic post on the Arkansas go up in the flames he himself would have to light—perhaps his recommendations would have been different and Fort St. Vrain would not have been built. However, not only did it come to be, but it would continue to be on the maps that Fremont made famous from 1843 on; for the next twenty years Fort St. Vrain was almost alone in the region to be so marked and to provide a focus, a stopover, a campground, a communications center, for decades to come.

Recalling Fort St. Vrain's landmark status, an early Colorado pioneer named Marshall Cook in a handwritten memoir entitled, "Early History of Colorado," wrote:

> The St. Vrain brothers [he is referring to Ceran and Marcellin] built Fort St. Vrain at the great Bend of the Platte on the south and east side, after the plan of all Mexican haciendas: a thick, high wall with watch towers at the diagonal corners for the protection of the wall and Fort, the tower being two stories high with the portholes through the wall, and a fireplace on the inside for the comfort of the watchman in cold weather. The walls of the fort composed a part of the building which were built inside of the main walls—the center of these enclosures was used to corrall the stock better to [defend] the post in times of danger and also with a well to furnish water in case of a seige and with an underground passage that was connected with the main building by a trap door the outside opening of the passage way was concealed by placing some split timber over the entrance with a light coat of earth that could be displaced from the inside to allow a party to escape under cover of darkness of night, in case they were about to be over powered by a foe superior in number. A huge gate for the admittance of the stock always was when occupied kept locked. If many of these old forts could talk what a history would have been [recited], especially Fort St. Vrain as before stated built by the St Vrains and occupied by them as a trading post while trading with the numerous tribes of Indians that frequented this part of the plains until a difficulty arose between the St. Vrains and the Araphoe Indians.

We note the crucial role of the elder Bent brothers (Charles, William and George) in the designing and actual

19

construction of Fort St. Vrain. But in the decades following Marshall Cook's account, the attributing of the fort to the St. Vrain's from beginning to end was the accepted opinion, and on the DAR monument of 1911 this is reflected in naming Ceran as the builder. He was, more precisely, a financier and building partner to start with.

In the narrative which follows Marshall Cook retells the "difficulty" which he learned about from a partially Anglicized Indian named Friday the Arapaho. To Marshall Cook, writing in 1880 of matters he learned in 1858-1862 or so, this account IS the story of Fort St. Vrain pertinent to an early history of Colorado. It is an account which has been relayed in other sources. LeRoy Hafen, the Colorado State Historian in 1952, includes it in his essay, "Fort St. Vrain," printed in the Colorado Historical Society's publication, *Colorado Magazine*, in October of 1952. Guy Peterson, in a monograph "The Four Forts of the South Platte" tells the tale also. Dean Kraken, in his Weld County history, *South Platte Country*, also repeats the story as does Hazel Johnson, Greeley historian, for a feature in the *Greeley Tribune*. All these editors decline comment, since there has not been corroboration of the story from independent historical sources. The question of its authencity is thus open. The following chapter about the history of Old Fort St. Vrain is an attempt to speak to this question.

ℕotes to Chapter Ⓞne
Bent's Fort of the South Platte

[1]David Lavender, *Bent's Fort*, Lincoln: Nebraska UP, 1972 [1954], 333.

[2]Lavender, 333.

[3]Frank Johnston, in his book for boys gives this description of pioneers building a sod house in *Old Tangle Eye*, Boston: Houghton-Mifflin, 1954, 64–67.

[4]Planning for the "Millenium Trails" project at the national level included the question, "Is the Old Trapper's Trail"—connected to both the Taos Trail and the Overland Trail—"part of the designated millenium trails?" The committe recommended the Old Trapper's Trail be designated an 'auxiliary' of the Overland Trail.

[5]George Hyde, *Life of George Bent: Written From His Letters,* Savoie Lottenville, ed., Norman: Oklahoma UP, 1983 [1968], 68.

[6]LeRoy Hafen, "Fort St. Vrain" in *Colorado Magazine,* October, 1952.

[7]Fred Gowan, *Rocky Mountain Rendezvous,* Provo: Brigham Young, UP, 1978, 197.

[8]In Wilber Stone's *History of Colorado* 1: 130.

[9]Lavender, 196–197.

[10]Howard Louis Conrad, *Uncle Dick Wootton; The Pioneer Frontiersman of the Rocky Mountain Region,* Lincoln: Nebraska UP, 1980 [1957], 82–83.

[11]Wootton credits the stage line owner Ben Holladay with creating the Pony Express but his editor Conrad notes that the freight-hauling company of Russell, Majors and Waddell, was the originator. Of course, the idea could have come from Fremont as well. See Conrad, 249.

[12]Francis Parkman, *Oregon Trail*. New York: [1849] 1993, 322–323.

[13]Quoted in Lee Whiteley, *The Cherokee Trail,* Boulder: Johnson Books, 1998, 74.

Chapter on early history
of Colorado

to the post in times of danger, and also with
a well to furnish water in case of a seige and
with an underground passage that was connected with
the main building by a trap door the out-side
opening of the passage way was concealed by placing
some split timber over the entrance, with a light-coat
of earth over, could be displaced from the inside
to allow a party to escape under cover of darkness, at
night incase they were about to be over power
by a foe superior in numbers. And has a gate for
the admittance of the stock which was always
occupied kept locked. If many of these old Forts
could talk what a history would have been written
especially Fort St. Vrain as before stated built
by the St. Vrains — and occupied by them a
a trading post, with the numerous Indians that
frequented these part of the plains until a difficulty
arose between the St. Vrain and the Arapahoe Indians
From what the writer could learn from an old Indian a Sub Chief known among the early settlers of
the Platte, Thompson, and the Poudre rivers, by the
name of old Friday who visited the Fort annually
until the last outbreak along the Platte, at this time resided
in the first settler of Northern Colorado When
Brush in the summer of 1868, when he
disappeared all of a sudden to join the main body
of his tribe. During his annual visit to the
Fort he would paint his face black. come

Page from Marshall Cook's "Early History of Colorado," about Old Fort St.
Vrain. Colorado Historical Society, Stephen Hart Library, Denver CO.

11. A Rather Fantastic Account

The preceding chapter described the establishment, personnel, and material history of Old Fort St. Vrain in the fur trade era. It concluded with an excerpt from an unpublished manuscript by an early pioneer, Marshall Cook, who came to northeastern Colorado in October, 1858 when this had been, since 1854, the westernmost edge of the Nebraska Territory. Writing in the early 1880's, near the end of his own lifespan in 1884, Cook remembered times of unrest when Nebraska Territorial government held no real sway over events hereabouts and when there was no actual "law and order." He also had read widely in the accounts of the mountain men in the central Rockies, in government reports and early histories, and he recalled the oral testimonies of persons who had been in the region since the first exploration of Stephen Long (1820). Cook had taken up a pre-emption claim of 160 acres near Old Fort St. Vrain and like so many others found the place mysterious and enchanting. Most important of all, he had lived through the terror of the Indian uprisings along the South Platte during the mid-to-late1860's—and the local climax of that anxious time—the killing of Ned Brush at the Brush ranch downstream along the South Platte. This event merged with the account he heard of the circumstances in which the St. Vrain manager abandoned Fort St. Vrain. His story's theme is the self-destructive lifestyle of the Indians who traded with the fort in the early days. Yet, lest the reader consider this introduction premature interpretation, let's look at Cook's narrative, and then consider some issues of its historicity.

[This account stems] from what the writer could learn from an old Indian or sub chief known among the early settlers of the Platte, Thompson and Poudre rivers, by the name of old Friday who visited Fort St. Vrain annually until the last outbreak along the Platte, [1868] at the time remembered by all the first settlers of northern Colorado—when Ned Brush was killed in the summer of 1868, when Friday disappeared all of a sudden to join the main branch of his tribe. During his annual visit to the Fort he would paint his face black, come and sit on the old walls and mourn and cry in a most deplorable manner. At times he would rend his excuse for clothing asunder and rave like a maniac and at others he would sway his body from side to side and howl like a wolf in the most agonizing lamentations. From him the writer learned the cause of his great sorrow. While the St. Vrains were trading at the old Fort that bears their name, they had occasion to go to St. Louis to dispose of their buffalo robes and peltries, preparatory to purchasing another stock of goods, leaving a squaw and child with some of Marcellin St. Vrain's countrymen and some Mexicans and some half breeds to look after the post during their absence, thinking no harm would befall this little band of adventurers as all the men were on friendly terms with Indians in the vicinity. . . . The St. Vrains felt well at ease and all went well till about the time that they were expected to return when a large party of Arapahoes assembled near the post to await their return, and some of the Arapahoes discovered that the squaw and child belonged to some other tribe that was a common enemy of theirs. The head chiefs of the Arapahoes called a council of the braves, in which it was decided to kill and scalp the squaw and her papoose to avenge some real or imaginary wrong received at the hands of the squaw's relatives. Consequently, the next day they carried out the decision and expression of the council by coming into the post pretending friendship, with their weapons concealed under their robes and blankets, overpowering the men and seizing the woman, dispatching her and the baby immediately, using in Friday's words, "kill 'em quick." St. Vrain's men buried their bodies inside of the post. The Arapahoes continued to stay in the vicinity of the Fort awaiting the St. Vrains' return thinking they

had done no harm by killing one or two of their common enemy and not taking into consideration that the child was near and dear, as likewise the mother, to one of the St. Vrains . . . who upon his arrival soon ascertained the sad state of affairs and as quickly decided to have revenge. He kept his own secrecies until he had his plans well matured, and not till the day of his revenge did he let his men know his intentions. . . . According to his customary role after returning from the east with a stock of goods, he invited all his customers to partake of a feast. In due time the feast was prepared but part of it in a very different manner to others which had been on previous occasions. He had the brass cannon that had accompanied the daring Frenchman on all occasions placed in one of the watch towers and well shotted for action, with nothing to do when all was in readiness but to apply the match, which would be the signal for human carnage to commence. He had provided plenty of ammunition at hand and assigned the piece to his regular gunner to command. His party was about 75 strong of able bodied men that were eager to wreak vengeance on the Indians for wrongs received at their hands—all well armed . . . placed in a secure position at the proper time with orders to fire into the Indians at a given signal. He had procured a fine fat elk, started a fire in the center of the fort and had the elk barbecued. The savory odor of the elk while cooking attracted the unsuspecting savages to gather around the post but [they]were not permitted to enter it. When all was about in readiness one of the young Indians on the outside of the post was sent to gather all the Indians old and young camped in the vicinity of the Fort to partake of the feast. The Indians soon collected, congratulating themselves on a sumptuous repast. When St. Vrain appeared before the gate he stated to them that as it was a social feast . . . none would be admitted with their fire arms. No one better understood the Indian nature or had more capacity to act on it than St. Vrain. . . . He was very particular to send the Indians word that one squaw and papoose was not much . . . and for them all to come and be merry (for he intended soon some of them shall die) and also that he wished to be friendly, in particular with those of the tribe that had slain his squaw and the child. At an early hour (as above stated) they gathered around the post; when all had assembled about the post and everything in readiness, he opened wide the gates so they could enter quickly which they lost no time in doing—little thinking of the death and devastation that awaited them. He extended them a cordial welcome and invited them (as they gathered around the feast which had been divided after it was sufficiently cooked and placed on boxes and endgates of wagon boxes) to help themselves. These rude tables were placed ranging with the cannon so that a raking shot would kill nearly the whole assemblage at the first fire. After all were in, the gates were casually closed and secured and so perfect was the stratagem that not the least suspicion was suspected on the part of the Indians—all being ready when the devastating match was applied. When the smoke had sufficiently cleared away it was seen that more than half of the reds had fallen. The cannon had mowed a road through the living mass of human beings killing or crippling all in its scope, . . . the devastating fire of the small arms nearly completing the work of destruction. So sudden was the surprise and so terrifying the shock that those of the Indians that had escaped the first fire were so paralyzed as seemingly to be unable to move a hand or foot, but by the time they began to recover from their lethargy, the trappers and teamsters employed by St. Vrain poured another round of deadly fire into the almost paralyzed Indians which fully aroused them to their situation and [they] were thrown into the wildest confusion. Then a hurried scramble commenced to see who could scale the walls. A few of the most active only succeeded in getting over . . . among those that made their escape was Friday, leaving his whole family to be numbered among the dead. The slaughter was kept up until all was killed; . . . most of the squaws and children fell on the first fire—the second finished the remainder. St. Vrain immediately cast the bodies into the well until it was full and piled the remainder in one corner of the corall, covered the pools of blood with the dry manure that had accumulated in the corral part of the fort. While some brought in and coralled the stock others loaded the wagons and they vacated the post during the night and traveled day and night until they crossed the divide at the head of cherry creek [and] did not waste much time until they

26

reached Bent's Fort where they found Bent and a large party of trappers and traders which they accompanied into New Mexico. Friday and his companions lost no time till they mounted their ponies and set out of the main village of the Arapahoes, which was at the mouth of Beaver Creek some 80 or 90 miles [of] distance, down the Platte. After relating what had happened to his party and resting for the night, they returned with a large party of warriors under the head chief to the Fort. To their chagrin the post was vacated and Friday found part of his family in the fire and part in the well. With the assistance of his friends and comrades they collected the bodies of their friends and relatives and conveyed them to the north side of the Platte river and buried them on a point of land about a mile west of B.H. Hew's house and sheep ranch—where they rested in place until the winter of 1869 and '70 when workers constructing the Julesburg railroad bed [uncovered them]. The bones were unearthed by John M. Hews, a contractor on that part of the road. And thus ends the early history of old Fort St. Vrain, and a fatal and mournful event on the part of the Arapahoes. These Indians were the beings of self-provoked destruction, a cold blooded murder committed on their part on a harmless squaw and child, and for no reason only that they belonged to another tribe—an enemy[1] .

Cook's manuscript was known to exist far before it was made public. At the turn of the century, Francis Cragin wrote in his own "Early West Notebooks" that he had tried to obtain a copy in the 1880-s or 90's and was unable to do so.

According to LeRoy Hafen in his 1952 article on Fort St. Vrain, this is:

> . . . the story of a tragedy that is said to have occurred at Fort St. Vrain. The story appears rather fantastic and we have found no contemporary records or accounts to substantiate it. It was written by Marshall Cook, a well known pioneer who came to Colorado in the gold rush and was one of the founders in 1858 of Arapahoe City, located on Clear Creek, about two miles east of Golden. He says the story was told him by Chief Friday of the

27

Arapahoes. Friday was the educated Indian whom
Thomas Fitzpatrick, famous fur man and Western
guide, had found as a boy and took back [to St. Louis] to
be educated in white man schools (251).

Then, Cook's daughter Mrs. Clingenspeel of Johnstown,
Colorado donated the manuscript to the Colorado Historical
Society in 1936. There it remained rather obscurely until
LeRoy Hafen published part of it in his essay about Fort
St. Vrain in 1952. Since then, paraphrased versions of this
account have appeared in several sources in state and local
publications. No subsequent records to date have verified this
"rather fantastic" account outright. Thus, the question I am
most frequently asked about Old Fort St. Vrain concerns this
story which is sensational enough to be remembered. Did
such an atrocity actually occur at Old Fort St. Vrain?

State and local historians have been, as I was initially,
very skeptical. As an exception, Virginia Trenholm,[2] in her
history of the Arapaho Indians, recommends the credibility
of the story on the grounds that "Marshall Cook was a reliable pioneer." Indeed, but his credibility is not the only question. At issue is not only Marshall Cook's rendition and
intention but Friday's command of English, his reliability as
the teller of the tale within the tale.

As Hafen pointed out, the story lacks corroboration and
sounds implausible, two difficulties in general with assessing
the story of the massacre as presented by Marshall Cook.
And yet, both Cook and Friday the Arapaho were well-known
figures in the early history of Colorado and both were known
for integrity and sobriety. Marshall Cook was the first pro-
bate judge of Arapaho County, Kansas Territory, in 1858. He
maintained an impressive record of public service throughout his lifetime. Friday was one of the few Arapaho Indians
who knew enough English to mediate problems between the
Anglos and the Arapaho. This was a service he did provide,
however, and the price he paid was to be criticized by both
sides. Perhaps, as he narrated his great sorrow to Marshall
Cook, that was among the reasons for it.

While the majority of the plains Indian population remain anonymous in European-immigrant histories, Friday the Arapaho was well remembered. During the 1860's Friday led a small band which frequently resided along the Cache la Poudre river or the Big or Little Thompson rivers in northern Weld and central Larimer counties. He had been, for a time, an adopted son of Thomas "Broken Hand" Fitzpatrick, the greatly respected mountain man and Indian agent who worked diligently in the late 1840's, early 1850's, at the newly created Upper Platte and Arkansas Indian Agency to secure rights for Indians and security for emigrants.

Many years prior to his tenure as Indian agent, while Fitzpatrick was head of the Rocky Mountain Fur Company, he discovered, in 1831, a five year old Arapaho boy lost along the Cimarron cutoff of the Santa Fe Trail. The thirty-two year old Fitzpatrick took him in, naming him Friday for the day on which he had been found. Friday accompanied his new guardian to Fort Laramie, the company's headquarters at that time, and in the fall to St. Louis, where Fitzpatrick enrolled him in school. In this way Friday learned the English language and European values and culture.

Nearly two years later, St. Louis merchant Robert Campbell, Fitzpatrick's close friend and erstwhile business partner, brought the seven or eight year old boy back to the Rocky Mountain region. Friday made a second journey to St. Louis soon after, in 1833, with Fitzpatrick. The party included William M. Anderson, who noted Friday's "astonishing memory, his minute observations, . . . his amusing inquiries." Anderson also remarked that Friday, whose Indian name was "Warshinum," meaning "Black Spot," recalled many of his tribe's fireside anecdotes.

Friday's immersion in white culture came to an end eventually, for the boy's Indian parents heard about a rescued lad and persisted in their efforts to have Fitzpatrick's Arapaho boy returned to them. Somewhat reluctantly, Friday met with his parents, was reunited with his Indian family, and remained with them. Once he achieved adulthood, he returned to St. Louis several times to visit his friends there.

In the year leading up to the landmark treaty of 1851, designed and executed by Thomas Fitzpatrick as Indian agent, Friday was among a delegation who traveled to Washington, D.C. to speak with government officials about the benefits of the proposed treaty.[3]

In the intervening years, Friday moved with his band about the plains. Twice he surprised Thomas Fitzpatrick during the latter's career as a scout and frontier guide during the 1840's. In July of 1843, Friday's small group encountered Fitzpatrick, who was acting as guide for John Charles Fremont's second expedition to the Rocky Mountain region and points west. Friday traveled with the expedition for three days before affectionately bidding his benefactor farewell. Two years later, Friday again met up with Fitzpatrick who was guiding a Kearny military expedition to South Pass near the Oregon Trail. At Lodge Pole Creek in southeastern Wyoming, Fitzpatrick was amazed to find Friday with his Arapaho companions. LeRoy Hafen says that Kearny's soldiers were astounded at the sight of their stern, impassive guide greeting an Indian warrior with sincerest demonstrations of affection.[3]

Friday ended his days at the Wind River reservation in Wyoming. Despite the fact that he had refused to fight against the whites—and was showered with contempt by Indian warriors for this reason—Friday and his group were shunted there at the insistence of Weld and Larimer whites who were intolerant of all unfettered Indian presences. His knowledge of English made him often the only one who could deal with the whites on behalf of his tribe. Whites, of course, wanted to see all mediators as "Chiefs," as one who had the power and authority to make deals stick, but Friday denied himself this title, perhaps because he had refused to join the fighting Indians. So Marshall Cook is accurate in dubbing him a "sub-chief." Friday died May 13, 1883, and was remembered as a valuable interpreter for the U.S. Army and other government agencies, an Indian who had dealt with wisdom and restraint in situations extremely difficult and unrewarding.

One of the early travelers along the South Platte, Rufus Sage, a writer who worked for a time at Lupton's Fort, found himself in a St. Louis bound group in 1844. Among them was Friday, who was then about eighteen. Sage, too, found Friday praiseworthy for "honesty, integrity and sobriety" as well as for hunting and other frontier skills. Sage recalled that Friday helped relieve camp boredom with his "vast fund of ready anecdotes and amusing stories." Friday, then, was a natural-born storyteller, and Cook's experience as a listener in Friday's presence dovetails perfectly with that of other whites. Friday must have enjoyed the attention he received in this way and the implied acceptance by his white audience. After 1846, his stories probably reflected less amusement and more tragedy, but this, too, is consistent with the history of the area once the whites began to sweep through and then, in ever greater numbers, to settle permanently to farm and ranch. As his destiny unfolded, Friday was not accepted by the whites but was, rather, just another Indian who had to be contained on a reservation.

So, Friday indeed told Marshall Cook a story about his extended Arapaho family, and the deaths of some of them at Fort St. Vrain. Their conversations probably took place sometime between 1860, when Marshall Cook came to the St. Vrain valley, and 1869 as we surmise because after 1870 Friday lived on the Wind River Reservation at Fort Washakie in present Wyoming. Cook, like Friday, enjoyed the role of storyteller, and he embellished Friday's story in his paraphrasing of it. Certain problems with the adaptation immediately appear. There is a shift in the tone of the story owing to Cook's interpretation and framing of Friday's account, resulting in an emotional atmosphere quite different than Friday's *grief*. Sometimes, Cook's account is delivered with relish, as when he describes the care with which the cannon was "well shotted," and St. Vrain's calculation as he savored his revenge. Friday could not have known these details when the event occurred. Would he have imagined them with such satisfaction later?

There is also a question of Friday's English, which must have been limited; furthermore, the cultural gaps between the Plains Indians' lifestyle—its "Archaic" social realities, (as the anthropologists tell us) versus the technologically more advanced Anglo culture—make some ideas literally untranslatable. For example, family relationships—kinship—are so different that language can't account for some of them. An idea like "sister" has a broad significance among Indians and so does "wife." In English these words signify something more official, monogamous and limited. Anglos heard these approximations and thought they understood when they could not quite truly do so because the cultural structures in Indian families were not the same as theirs. Another example may be found in Friday's phrase "kill 'em quick." Marshall Cook says this is a direct quote about the woman and baby the Arapaho killed, allegedly the wife and child of St. Vrain's manager, Marcellin. When I first read Cook's account, this didn't mean much to me, but now I suspect this refers to a *merciful* dispatching of the enemy as opposed to a slow, torturous death. It may have been a kind of apology and defense on Friday's part, if he meant to tell Cook that the executions could have been worse.

Marshall Cook adds detail and creates a "subtext" (an implied narrative, read "between the lines") by referring to the Indian depredations when Ned Brush was murdered at his compound in 1868. This is actually Marshall Cook's emphasis. Friday the Arapaho provides a grim anecdote about St. Vrain's revenge over a murdered squaw and papoose. Cook uses it as an example of the way Indians themselves provoked whites to obliterate their culture. Ned Brush's death, to Cook, is one more example on a long list of completely counter-productive Indian actions.

Although we now see that those Indian warriors who killed Ned Brush in 1868 were reacting, despairingly, tragically, to the massacre of Black Kettle's band at Sand Creek, Cook assumes the habitual villainy of the Indians saying that St. Vrain "well knew their character," and acted appropriately on his insight. If Cook meant that the Arapaho characteristically killed their enemies—not personal enemies but any member of an enemy group as a symbol of the whole—

then he had justification proven by many sources both white and Indian.

Thus, Friday's history is told to Cook to explain his great sadness but Cook's motives differ; his "occasion"—what prompts a narrator to tell a story—is, in part at least, the killing of Ned Brush in 1868, the worst of "Indian depredations" along the South Platte and the cause of ferocious white outrage. Both are subsumed within the pervading theme of the Indians' self-destructive policies. Cook emphasized the Brush slaying; this was what area settlers remembered about the early history of northeastern Colorado— while Friday the Arapaho had no reason to place the 1868 incident in his anecdote. In this way we reasonably suppose that Cook's history of Fort St. Vrain was written not only out of his pity for Friday but on his understanding that Friday's fellows brought this exile upon themselves and on one another. Friday probably agreed.

Eventually I came to agree with Virginia Trenholm. Cook was a reliable pioneer, making a valid point. I also came to believe that Friday was a reliable narrative source even though language barriers could have created misunderstanding. Something awful did happen at Fort St. Vrain which Marcellin's family would recall as his "trouble with the Indians." Cook's account of Friday's memoir is one explanation of what that trouble was. In independent accounts, according to Marcellin St. Vrain there was trouble, but it was a trivial misunderstanding, an accidental death of one Indian resulting from a wrestling match to which his relatives overreacted. Neither explanation seems altogether plausible. It was the implausible feel of these stories which caused LeRoy Hafen to describe Cook's account as "rather fantastic." Just how fantastic is it?

Marcellin St. Vrain's men allegedly threw Indian bodies into the well at Old Fort St. Vrain after the massacre. The Indians returned to the fort and retrieved their dead from the well. A story persisted that the well at Old Fort St. Vrain was polluted, not by dead bodies, but by a cannon. A relatively early pioneer to this area, Orpha McNitt, who came as a post-Civil War bride, spent a fourth of July, 1871 near Fort St. Vrain, and recalled exploring the premises: "I had heard of an old well where a canon [sic] had been dumped, but I couldn't find it."[4] And, in 1952 when the site at Fort St. Vrain was threatened by area ranching activity, the Colorado State Historian, LeRoy Hafen, traveled to the site prior to publishing his summary of documents relative to it in the fur trade era. Hafen's publicity was channeled through the *Rocky Mountain News,* July 25, 1952 which carried the headline "Dispute is Raging Over Leveling of Old Fort Site Near Denver." Under the sub-topic "Cannon Reported Hidden," Hafen was quoted as saying a "visitor to the fort reported that an old brass cannon was tossed into the fort well to hide it during an Indian attack."[5] The only attack we can surmise ever occurred would have been the search for vengeance described by Friday. The rumor that there had been a cannon in the well may have been based on a folk memory confusion. The shift from victims of destruction, Indians, to the reputed agent of destruction, reverses outright the protagonist and antagonist in the story. Now the Indians are the aggressors and the whites are on the defensive. Since the story is being told by whites, isn't that how it ought to be?

It is possible, however, that this rumor also arose out of a confusion between Bent's Fort on the Arkansas and Bent's on the South Platte. When William Bent destroyed Old Bent's Fort in 1849, he exploded gunpowder and, quite possibly, threw an old and dysfunctional brass cannon down the well to prevent "squatters" from capitalizing on his hard work and dedication to his "adobe castle" on the plains. If this is the historical basis for the tradition that held a cannon had been tossed down the well at Fort St. Vrain, it exists side by side with the folklore dynamics whereby the cannon displaced the bodies in folk memory, conveniently turning the Arapaho victims into the attackers and relieving the whites of guilt for the death of Indians. The cannon became not an agent of destruction but a sacrifice given to a watery grave, and the whites would be more or less defenseless without it.

Most importantly, both symbols belong to a common motif: whether the well contains the victims or the weapon of death, THE WELL WAS POISONED. The only argument concerns who was to blame.

Doubt may also be cast on aspects of Cook's account using grounds of plausibility or verisimilitude. This criterion involves questions of what we expect from our knowledge of the usual way of the world—"common sense"— and facts arrived at through corroboration from several reliable sources. For example, the Arapaho customarily buried their dead in trees or placed them on rigged scaffolding until only the bones remained. These would then be buried. In Cook's account, the Arapaho retrieved their dead from the well at Fort St. Vrain and also from the corall and promptly buried them. It is not clear why they would have made this exception, and perhaps Marshall Cook assumed the universality of white customs regarding the burial of the dead.

Another question arises regarding the cannon. Truly, one could have been loaded with shrapnel and set in the bastion.[6] But the firing of a raking shot would have been severely limited through the gunwale, even if a loophole did point to the interior instead of the exterior of the fort. The space in the bastion was so cramped that the "kick" of the cannon might have unloosed the adobe bricks behind it. In this tight space, the kick might also have maimed the gunner.

Cook is careful to describe the means by which the Indians were disarmed. No firearms were allowed inside the fort's premises where the barbecue promised a somber end: "eat drink and be merry for tomorrow you shall die." Surely Friday the Arapaho did not say precisely this to Cook; the likelihood that he knew of the ancient Epicurean Greek philosopher's maxim is small, but that he would have applied it to the situation of his clan members in these circumstances is unthinkable. In 1844 or 1846 when this event might have actually occurred, the Indians had no firearms, or very few. In those years, they were almost always strictly a bow-and-arrow foe. And under no circumstances would they be welcome into the fort with weapons. Commercial forts had

Dutch doors to deal with people who for one reason or another ought to stay outside.

Some sources of Indian history tell us that the Arapaho were terrified of this particular armament, a cannon.[7] Would commercial forts have displayed prominently a piece of equipment which would have interfered with peaceable trading practices—their reason for existence—and might have driven off their clientele? The National Park Service interpreters at Bent's Fort on the Arkansas contend that a one-pound cannon was placed on the rooftops of the two corner bastions at Old Bent's Fort, but that since the fort was never attacked, these were used only to fire warning shots or mark a holiday celebration. Research files in the library suggest that these might have been the type used by Spanish ships, mounted on the railings in the great Armada of the 1500's. They could fire directly at a target with a ball or, loaded with shrapnel, scatter-shot, as in Cook's account, to ward off pirates or otherwise protect their navy.

However, the early West was not militarized in the early 1840's. The War Department seems to have enforced policies forbidding civilians to commandeer such heavy artillery. Only after General Kearny's Army of the West used Bent's Old Fort as a jumping-off place for a United States war against Mexico was there any permanent or semi-permanent military presence in southeastern Colorado. Thus, it is likely that the cannon at Bent's Fort was put in place during or after 1846.

William Bent's son George recalled that an old brass cannon, damaged during a misfire, lay about the grounds, accumulating rust.[8] When William Bent decided to leave Bent's Fort for good and left his family in the wagon, returning literally to blow up his marvelous trading post, he concentrated on damaging the well, since his purpose was to create difficulties for any would-be trader squatters to take over the facility and benefit from his hard work without effort on their own part. This brass cannon was then tossed into the well with other refuse, and with a keg of gunpowder, says George Bent, exploded. This left an indelible connection in the minds of later historians and archaeologists, between an old brass cannon and an explosion in a well. Would not the first have caused the second? "Poisoning the well" is a folklore motif. In modern times of public water systems, the phrase is a metaphor for a vicious but common practice of destroying another person's reputation—disempowering a rival—by spreading negative gossip behind the back. In the unsettled times of the West in the 1840's it meant something more literal, but also a pre-emptive measure against potential rivals.

Supposing there was really a cannon among Fort St. Vrain's defenses, we believe it would have been brought there no earlier than 1844 or 1845, after Fremont's second visit of 1843. A more significant detail in Cook's account concerns the small arms fire that supplemented the cannon shot. The source might have been a type of battery gun which was a forerunner of the Gatling. Friday, who was in the midst of the terror and was busy scaling the fort walls, might not have been the best witness as to whether the attack came from repeating rifles. If the cannon was in the loft of the bastion as the story says, hidden from view, the Indians probably did not know exactly what was being fired.

Whether the former, more plausible, interpretation, is nearer the truth—or, less likely, whether a cannon really was fired off—it seems plausible that the event was not completely a figment of Friday's imagination but that in the shock and confusion he may not have had the minor details so clearly in mind. Therefore, I believe that some Arapaho Indians were killed— more than 6 but less than 30—some like Friday escaped, and some returned for vengeance days later. Finding the fort "deserted," at least of its white occupants (Marcellin's wife and three children may have hidden for safety, gone with him to Bent's Fort, or been sent to stay with Sioux family members near Fort Laramie), the Indians tore the entry gates off their hinges and left the fort in some chaos—the situation observed by Francis Parkman a few weeks later. By this time, Spotted Fawn seems to have been at Fort St. Vrain, as will be explained subsequently.

A veteran employee of the Bent St. Vrain Co., Uncle Dick Wootton, wrote in his autobiography a fascinating chapter that tells of his settling in 1862 near old Fort Pueblo, with land aplenty since there were so few people in the platted settlement. Why were the opportunities so open at the town that would become Pueblo, Colorado? Uncle Dick explains:

> The massacre which had occurred in 1854 had operated to keep people away from there, not only because they feared another outbreak but because they had a sort of superstitious dread of being near the old fort. The walls of the old adobe building had been stained and bespattered with the blood of the victims of the slaughter and there were stories about its being haunted, which made even some of the mountain men timid about stopping over night in it when they passed that way[9] .

Wootton recalls a similar instance of avoidance based on a history of violence at a spot southeast of Denver called Fagan's camp, and tells how he exploded the superstition by accidentally sleeping on the grave of the murdered man. The inquiring reader, if he or she is given to analysis by analogies, may wonder, then, if the bloodshed at Fort St. Vrain would have engendered the same traditions of ghost story and haunted forts, and taboo. Was its reported "abandonment" evidence of atrocity? If so, why were there no ghost stories about old Fort St. Vrain such as there were about old Fort Pueblo? Perhaps because no massacre actually happened, one may suppose. Only after further study does one consider a point of contrast: at Fort St. Vrain, the victims were *Indians*. Perhaps that has made all the difference!

The plausible interpretation is that Friday recalled the events most probably of the spring or summer of 1846 just before Marcellin left Fort St. Vrain for Bent's Fort, amid Marcellin's "trouble with the Indians" which Bent, St. Vrain Company spokesmen, or perhaps only Marcellin himself, described as a wrestling match in which one Indian was killed. Friday's version is more convincing. Marcellin weighed about 115 pounds and is not likely to have "accidentally" killed any opponent in a wrestling match. That he would have ordered fort employees to fire upon a group of Indians is not, in itself, out of the question, but his reason for doing so is somewhat puzzling. For, the only wife and "papoose" that we know of at Fort St. Vrain, whose murder he was avenging, lived long and quite well documented lives. Marshall Cook would not have known this, however, in the 1880's. This problem will be more fully addressed in the following chapter about the life and family of Marcellin St. Vrain.

In Cook's pioneer experience, construction workers eventually discovered a "mass grave" while creating a railroad bed for "the Julesburg railroad" on land owned then—the 1870's—by one John Hewes, perhaps the same as an early census of 1860 names Jno. Hughes. He was associated with the building of an irrigation ditch and was, in 1867, in partnership with Cook on the #13 ditch. In effect, this puts Marshall Cook in a perfect position to have witnessed himself the unearthing of these bodies. How he knew they were the same as those buried from an atrocity at Fort St. Vrain is not clear, but it was reasonable for him to assume that not many mass graves existed completely unaccounted for in the region's traditional lore.[10]

In conclusion, it must be admitted that the most compelling reason to dismiss Cook's story is the lack of corroboration. Not only does the absence of an independent account deprive the manuscript of its value as a *scientific* document—proven—but a general reader, applying common sense analysis, will expect that an event so evidently appalling would have circulated among the company employees or the St. Vrain family or Arapaho Indians and their historians and leaked out in at least one other source: folk tales of horror, diaries, letters, or other historical accounts. We are inclined to suppose that such a widespread conspiracy of silence is impossible, and that the events, then, must not have really occurred outside of Friday the Arapaho's vivid imagination. The story is merely a record of the kind of nightmares engendered by the paranoia of Anglos and Indians vis a vis one another. Or is it? In the next chapter we will consider some circumstantial evidence that Marcellin St. Vrain did some harm to Arapahos at Fort St. Vrain.

ℕotes to Chapter 𝒯wo
A *Rather Fantastic* Account

[1]Marshall Cook, Unpublished manuscript, "Early History of Colorado," Colorado Historical Society, Stephen Hart Library, 125–131.

[2]Virginia Trenholm, *The Arapahoes, Our People,* Norman: Oklahoma UP, 1970, 151–52.

[3]This account of Friday stems from LeRoy Hafen's biography of Thomas Fitzpatrick; *Broken Hand: The Life of Thomas Fitzpatrick, Mountain Man, Guide and Indian Agent,* Lincoln: Nebraska UP, 1973 [1931], 325–36. This quote stems from an appendix "Friday the Arapaho," 327.

[4]Orpha McNitt, *Letters From a Frontier Bride,* Emma Alice Hamm, editor, self-published, 1993, 50.

[5]*Rocky Mt. News* July 25, 1952.

[6]If it were a small cannon, Spanish-made, used on ships, it could be loaded with fragments. The howitzer, however, shot one shell. It is not clear what Cook has in mind in his claim about "a raking shot."

[7]As discussed in LeRoy Hafen's biography of Thomas Fitzpatrick, Hafen quotes Francis Parkman describing Arapaho reaction to a howitzer: ". . . many of the Arapahos fell prostrate to the ground, while others ran screaming with amazement and terror. On the following day they withdrew . . . confounded with awe at the appearance of the Dragoons, at their big gun which went off twice at one shot [the howitzer threw a shell] . . ." Quoted from Chapter 16 in Parkman's *The California and the Oregon Trail* and found in Hafen's *Broken Hand,* 216.

[8]See George Hyde, *Life of George Bent,* 85. George Bent recalls that Kearny's army of 1846 was greeted like royalty at Bent's Fort: ". . . as the General rode up at the head of the column a salute was fired from a brass howitzer on the walls of the fort, but the gun burst. For many years this old brass gun lay in the main court of the fort."

[9]Howard Conrad's biography of Uncle Dick Wootton, Chapter 25, "The Haunted Fort" 270.

[10]Bones of slain Indians, as well as mammoths have been found near a railroad bed adjacent to the Fort St. Vrain Power Generating Plant. The famous Dent site remains an important archeological and paleontological site today. What Marshall Cook witnessed may or may not be the same bones Friday refers to.

Marcellin St. Vrain, manager of Fort St. Vrain 1838-1846. Courtesy of St. Vrain Power Generating Plant.

III. The Booshway of
Fort St. Vrain

he central character of Marshall Cook's story is "the
St. Vrain," the one who avenged his family's murders
at the feast described in the previous chapter. Apparently Cook did not know Marcellin's first name. The connection between the manager at Fort St. Vrain and the young
Marcellin is indisputable, though. This chapter will assume
the connection with Cook's central character to the young
Marcellin and will focus on biographies of him and his Fort St.
Vrain family as a way of responding to a question: How did
the character of Marcellin St. Vrain affect the history of Old
Fort St. Vrain?

During Fort St. Vrain's "fur trade era," the years 1837-
1846, when it was actively involved in transactions with the
Indians, primarily for buffalo hides and fur products,
Marcellin St. Vrain was in charge. In 1838, when the fort was
completed, Marcellin was just twenty-two years old, but he
carried the power and responsibilities of a much older, more
seasoned, man. His title as booshway came about as follows:
the British (i.e., the Hudson Bay Company) called their trade
managers "factors," while the French termed theirs the "bourgeois." The slangy, multi-national mountain men pronounced
"bourgeois"—literally 'middle-man'— as "booshway." The factor or booshway was, like a sea captain, a king in the wilderness and within the confines of his business and his post, his
word was absolute. Today, also, the hundreds of American families who congregate to celebrate a "Rendezvous" and reenact

those first county fairs of the west, soon learn that the boosh-way,. by rights and traditions, interprets the rules and what he decides, goes. However, a booshway was also an Indian trader by profession and as one writer stated the matter was fated to be "the victim of a myth."[1] Thus, his role as empire-builder and the potential for tragedy in his lifestyle created an ironic tension for men like Marcellin St. Vrain.

This booshway of Fort St. Vrain was born into a distin-guished French-Catholic Missouri family on October 14, 1815, the youngest of ten children born to Jacques Marcellin Ceran de Hault de Lassus de St. Vrain—and his wife Marie Felicite. The family resided at their estate near Spanish Lake in St. Louis County.

Marcellin was, in all the ways a young American in the west could be, well-connected. The detailed genealogy of his ancestors relates that his paternal grandfather had been advisor to Louis the XVI, in the years before the Revolution of 1789, and liaison from the King to the French Parliament. His grandfather emigrated to America in the bloody after-math of '89, while two sons, Charles and Jacques, (Jacques was Marcellin's father) served as officers in the French Navy during their late teens, and in Spain for four years or so. Having acquired valuable training and connections during service in Spain, Marcellin's father took up a naval career along the Mississippi. Paul St. Vrain, in his family history published in the 1940's explains that ". . . after coming to this country he [Jacques] was given command of whatever navy vessels the Spanish had in the Mississippi River."[2] Marcellin's uncle, Charles Auguste de Lassus (he decided not to bear the St. Vrain title) eventually "was made Lieutenant Governor of Upper Louisiana Territory and officiated at the transfer of that domain to France [from Spain] and also from France to the United States in 1804" (i).

Of the sons of Jacques and Marie St. Vrain,, Ceran St. Vrain earned the greatest distinctions for pioneering the set-tlement of eastern Colorado and northern New Mexico through his role as a senior partner in the vast and success-ful "cartel", the Bent, St. Vrain Trading Co. Although the title "Colonel" was generally honorary only, not a regular military rank, Ceran lived up to the traditions of soldierly conduct, serving gallantly in the armed services during the turbulent times of the 1846 Mexican War and in the months following the bloody Taos uprising of 1847, in which his business partner and boyhood friend Charles Bent was murdered. Serving with distinction, Ceran earned his title.

Marcellin was nearly 13 year younger than Ceran. As the baby of the family, he was probably doted upon by a horde of aunts, uncles, older siblings as well as parents. He was given the best education available as befitted his aristocratic heritage. At age fifteen he entered (what is today known as) St. Louis University where he remained for two years. Whether his higher education was a hindrance or a help to him in his career in the untamed regions of the Rocky Mountain west is a matter for speculation. At first glance, elegant manners appear a waste, but the fortunate coincidence of John Charles Fremont's friendship with Marcellin at Fort St. Vrain belies such an assumption. Both at home and in school, he learned to present himself in the same mode that merited a description of manners attributed to his elder brother, Ceran: "Mr. St. Vrain was a gentleman in the true sense of the term, his French descent imparting an exquisite, indefinable degree of politeness . . ." (St. Vrain 7 quoted from *Wah-to-yah* by Lewis Garrard). Similarly, J.C. Fremont noted that Marcellin received his exploratory contingent, "graciously," with "customary kindness." Furthermore, as we shall see, Fremont could be a powerful ally and some of Marcellin's fame is owing to Fremont's friendship for him. In other ways, however, a college-educated gentleman must have found subtle communication difficult with a non-English speaking wife and employees who could be rowdy and recalcitrant. In other words, life at Fort St. Vrain entailed some "culture shock" and a great deal of adaptability.

In 1838, Marcellin St Vrain assumed his position along the South Platte River, the route long known as the Trappers' Trail. His eldest brother Ceran had settled into the business at Taos, and later at Mora, north of present Las Vegas, New

Mexico to service the trade between Santa Fe and Bent's Fort. Meanwhile the other senior partner Charles Bent traveled to and from St. Louis with the wagon trains. The Taos Trail was, thus, the byway for trade goods via the southern route, from St. Louis to Mexican towns and from there over the environs of Raton Pass to Bent's Fort along the Arkansas River, and on to the outpost Fort St. Vrain on the South Platte. From the site of Old Pueblo (Hardscrabble), to Fort Laramie, the Trappers' Trail described the road along the eastern slope of the central Rocky Mountains that gave the "beaver men" access to fur trading posts near and far. Thus, the Taos and Trappers' trails overlapped, at least as far as Fort Laramie.

The first year that Marcellin managed Old Fort St. Vrain, the seasoned mountaineers Peter Sarpy and Henry Fraeb from Fort Jackson ten miles upstream offered to purchase the buffalo robes he had received from the Cheyenne, Arapaho and perhaps Sioux Indians and had pressed, baled and stored— ten robes to a bale, as the custom was. Marcellin agreed—whether from naivete, temporary incapacity owing to drink, immaturity, or pure loneliness, we do not know. But when the season ended, and it was time to load company furs onto the wagons or boats bound for Missouri, the booshway at Fort St. Vrain had almost nothing to show but $32 from Fraeb and Sarpy, managers of Fort Jackson. Doubtless they had the entire neighborhood chuckling over their 19th century version of one-upmanship.

Elder brother Ceran was not amused. The next time he was in St. Louis, he dropped in on Fort Jackson's creditors, bought up their debts, and sold Fort Jackson to the Bent, St. Vrain Co. He notified William Bent of the acquisition and William Bent turned up at Fort Jackson to let the owners know that they were no longer in business. Shortly thereafter, a list of the goods transferred to Fort St. Vrain by the now defunct Sarpy and Fraeb enterprise etched the mini-drama forever in Western American history. In spite of the greenhorn antics of their main outpost's manager, the Bent, St. Vrain company had saved face. The wooden stockade of Fort Jackson (it was near another Trappers' Trail ghost town marked on the highway maps as the town of Ione) was burnt to the ground. William Bent was not about to allow more competition in his back yard and so Fort Jackson had be destroyed rather than remain a windfall for some would-be entrepreneur.

Poor Henry Fraeb was killed in an Indian battle not long after this buy-out. Peter Sarpy went to work at other posts of the American Fur Company and was hounded out of the West by U.S. government enforcers of the laws against selling liquor to the Indians. Sarpy eventually returned to the family business in the bustling Missouri river town of Bellevue then overshadowing and just south of present Omaha—in what was yet to become Nebraska Territory. The Sarpy mercantile would become one of the links between the Colorado of the mountain men and traders and that of the gold seekers in 1858. These connections will be reviewed in a subsequent chapter.

Back at Fort St. Vrain, even a greenhorn of middling stature must benefit from the education his mountain man mentors make available to him. If Marcellin St. Vrain came to the wilderness of the Rockies for hero-worship of his older brother, he matured quickly in a school of hard knocks and the mountaineers and frontiersmen who befriended him respected his place within the great Bent, St. Vrain Co. partnership. He had first come west in his later 'teens, about 1833, much like the young William Bent who hurried more eagerly than any Huck Finn to traverse the Missouri River trading posts in the late 1820's. As William Bent traced his destiny according to the example of Charles, so Marcellin found his heart leaning toward the adventuresome life described by Ceran.

About 1838-1839, Marcellin married Spotted Fawn, a thirteen year old Sioux, said to be a relative of Red Cloud, a "sister." In the family tradition of the St. Vrains, she is "Royal." David Lavender comments (in his *Bent's Fort*) that this was pronounced "Rel." Not convinced that she was so named in mountain man or Franco-American accents, some chroniclers reported that she was called "Red,"—ostensibly for the highlights in her hair. Her grandson, W.R. Sopris, names her "Red" in his memoir of her published in *Colorado Magazine*, March, 1945. At some point, her nickname was probably revised and "Royal", "Rel" and "Red" are probably all correct for various periods of her life. It is not likely that her grandson W.R. would be incorrect, since his account comes from Spotted Fawn herself, but it seems that Marcellin called her "Rel." She was his royal Indian princess.

They had four children, according to the St. Vrain family genealogy. The first lived only eighteen days and remained unnamed. Felix St. Vrain was born June 17, 1842, at Fort St. Vrain. He died of smallpox, unmarried, in a Union Army prison at Vicksburg after having enlisted on the Confederate side at the outbreak of the Civil War. Charles St. Vrain was born October 17, 1844. at the Fort. His descendants are numerous, many still Colorado and New Mexico residents. The third child, Mary Louise St Vrain, was born March 9 or 10, 1846. She later claimed, whether out of vanity or ignorance, that she was born in 1848. But her brother Charles insisted to interviewer Francis Cragin in about 1903 that Mary Louise was two years younger than he. I have adopted this 1846 date as correct and therefore my timetable of events differs somewhat from David Lavender's who uses 1848. At any rate, her claim caused considerable confusion among historians who could not then date Marcellin's final departure from Fort St. Vrain accurately.

At Fort St. Vrain, the educated, elegant, mannered Marcellin discovered that tedious hours far outnumbered times of adventure. There was trading to be done, there were accounts to be kept, about twenty-five workers to oversee concerning livestock, procuring wild game, guarding the post, preparing meals, hauling goods, and baling hides. His wife, Spotted Fawn, tended a vegetable garden in which she took enormous pride. Upstream, the Cheyenne Indian wife of Lancaster Lupton, Thomass, carried on a lively competition with a large garden of her own. The area along the South Platte north of Denver has ever since been especially suited for "truck farming," an industry still predominant today. It is pleasing for modern residents of the South Platte Valley to recall that these Indian wives of the earliest traders and entrepreneurs founded this vital industry.

At Fort St. Vrain, occasionally, there would be white guests, hunters, guides, emigrants, to be housed and entertained, and sometimes Marcellin joined the hunting expeditions. Solomon Sublette from Fort Lupton and "Bap" Charbonneau who worked at Fort St. Vrain at least intermittently, recall including Marcellin on a hunt for bighorn sheep. But, despite David Lavender's claim that Marcellin loved hunting, Marcellin was only marginally excited by this sport. Joseph Walker, one of the best pathfinders of the American West, reported that Marcellin St. Vrain was left in charge of Bent's Fort during the 1846 campaign of Stephen Watts Kearny into Mexico. The Bent brothers accompanied the army as scouts. Walker's biographer, Bil Gilbert speaks of Walker's account:

> . . . Marcellus [the Latin form of his name] had always been a restless young man with no great interest in the routine business of the company, and found staying home and taking care of the store excruciatingly tedious. Therefore, when Walker told him that antelope were plentiful around his camp and invited him to come out for sport hunting, Marcellus accepted eagerly so as to "obtain relief from the close confinement of the fort." The game was abundant, as promised, but Marcellus found the sandflies were so fierce that he "little enjoyed the pleasure of hunting." Deciding he would rather be bored than bitten to death, he returned after spending a week as Walker's guest (Gilbert 223).

David Lavender dubbed Marcellin St. Vrain the "harum-scarum youngster." Stories about his antics include one memorable demonstration of antelope hunting. Marcellin tied a red cloth around one ankle, stood on his head in the prairie grass and waved his legs back and forth. Surely the antelope, curious as they were, would approach within shooting range to investigate this strange sight. This story was often retold— without noting that the common Indian custom for catching antelope involved creating just such a V-shaped trap, though on a much larger scale, using two columns of hunters. George Bent presents a sketch of an antelope trap (in the book about his life by George Hyde) so that there seems to have been method in Marcellin's madness, then, and his visual parody of the antelope hunt reveals M. St. Vrain's comic logic; in a later time period, he might have made a great cartoonist.

Annually, in late March or early April the caravan of wagons set out from St. Vrain's bound for Bent's Fort on the Arkansas. The train would not have been large—perhaps four or five wagons loaded mostly with buffalo hides, dried tongue and cord which was made from woven manes of buffalo. But the train would acquire additional members as it trekked southeast—probably one at Fort Vasquez seven miles south, another at Fort Lupton. Although these trading posts were "abandoned" by 1842, common sense suggests that the warm-in-winter adobe structures would not have gone altogether uninhabited. In the guide books of the 1850's outfitters for gold seekers assured travelers they were "good camps." One or two more wagons might have swelled the ranks at Cherry Creek and possibly another along Fountain Creek, near Castle Rock, Colorado, driven by traders who either had worked for Bent, St. Vrain Co. the previous winter on temporary locations or independent traders who decided to throw in their lot with the company caravan for safety's sake.

The caravan would have carried mail as well—letters left at St. Vrain's by travelers up the Trappers' Trail or carried by mountain men who happened to have been recently at Fort Laramie. Mail to the "States" was so happenstance in those early decades that the the Fort on the best known route from Fort Laramie on the Oregon Trail to Bent's Fort on the Santa Fe Trail was an established, if not yet official, point for the north-south postal exchange. A local tradition holds that several years after the official closure of Fort St. Vrain by the company in 1846, the fort was still a place for "spring rendezvous": this probably means that Fort St. Vrain was an identifiable gathering point for many traders and travelers bound from the northern Rockies after a long winter endured.

The caravan would have driven loose stock—horses, mules, cattle (oxen)—animals given as gifts or in trade plus those that were raised from birth on the rich natural grass along the South Platte River. Of course, these represented only some fraction of Fort St. Vrain's livestock. Breeding stock, the newly born, and any ailing would not be included. Most likely, individuals from among friendly Arapaho and Cheyenne Indians would be found in the group as well. They might have errands among their southern cousins at Bent's Fort or political missions on behalf of their clans. Perhaps some were returning to Bent's Fort after having accomplished errands among their northern relatives. And, because William Bent was well known as the "Little White Man" who ransomed captives, this spring caravan may well have included persons—usually women or children—who had been brought to Fort St. Vrain by mediating individuals; these would be restored to their families—Comanche, Kiowa, Apache, or white. The caravan was a moving encampment and when it reached Bent's Fort only a few days respite would be allowed before the greater caravan moved out toward Santa Fe where Ceran St. Vrain and perhaps Charles Bent as well awaited their arrival.

On the two hundred fifty mile journey from the South Platte to Bent's Fort, accomplished at not more than twenty miles a day, Marcellin St. Vrain would be "Captain of the Caravan." Once his party arrived at Bent's Fort, William Bent took charge. Concerning this climactic annual journey, William's son George recalled:

> . . . [my uncle] George was sometimes left in charge of the fort when my father went to St. Louis to sell his furs and lay in a new stock of goods. My father made this trip every year, leaving the fort usually in April and going with the wagon train to West port (now Kansas City). From here he went to St. Louis by boat, returning to the fort with the train in the fall. This trip to the Missouri River and back to the fort was over one thousand miles, and my father made the journey

every year from about 1832 to 1852. For about ten years after 1852 he made the trip twice each year.[3]

Sometimes, also, Marcellin St. Vrain was left in charge at Bent's Fort, but more often he traveled out to greet his family mentor Ceran and probably continued on to St. Louis where he found respite among civilized social gatherings from the "culture shock" induced by his small, isolated empire on the South Platte.

The scenario just recreated, based on custom, might have gone on indefinitely except that history is often "stranger than fiction." Sometime during 1846, probably by late July, Marcellin St. Vrain left Fort St. Vrain. Here begins a confusing story, poignant and sad, surrounding the breakup of Spotted Fawn's first marriage and Marcellin's Fort St. Vrain family.

Royal's story: Spotted Fawn was born to the clan of Red Cloud in 1825. In 1839, when she was thirteen, she married Marcellin St. Vrain, booshway of Fort St. Vrain. No records remain to explain whether this was accomplished in the Indian fashion of presenting five horses to the bride's family—or where, between Fort Laramie and Fort St. Vrain, the ceremony occurred. During the next 6 years, she bore him three surviving children. Mary Louise St. Vrain, the last born, (after Felix and Charles) recalled that her mother was 21 years old that spring of Mary's birth in March, 1846. That was the time the great trouble began. That summer Marcellin hurriedly left Fort St. Vrain, telling his young wife never to breathe a word of some difficulties he had had with the Arapaho Indians, and reassuring her, again and again, that he would return as soon as he possibly could. In August, Spotted Fawn began to watch for her husband's return as he had promised, ever more anxiously as the weeks went by and he did not appear.[4]

Other Bent, St. Vrain employees did return to spend the winter season of 1846-47 at Fort St. Vrain and among them was William Bransford. Marcellin's young Indian wife suited his fancy and he, believing her husband would not be returning, began to hope that she would marry him. According to

Francis Cragin's papers, Bransford, a Virginian from Lynchburg who had moved to Kentucky and then on to St. Louis, told Billy Adamson:

> In August, 1844, in St. Louis, I hired to the firm of Bent, St. Vrain & Co. who were about to start a wagon train across the plains with supplies for their stores in Taos and Santa Fe. After a long and tedious journey we reached our destination and were sent by our employers to the different trading posts, namely Fort St. Vrain on the [South] Platte, Bent's Fort on the Arkansas, and the posts on Red River [Fort Adobe].[5]

This tallies correctly with Bransford's later testimony during the Maxwell Land Grant trials, that he had worked at and around Fort St. Vrain from 1844 to 1849. Bransford reported that by traveling to and from the posts he became personally acquainted with "all the early settlers," Lucien Maxwell, Ceran St. Vrain, General Kearny, and Governor Charles Bent. Cragin says Bransford was "honest, sincere, benevolent and had no enemies."

Spotted Fawn refused him, however, certain that her husband would return. In the book *Bent's Fort,* David Lavender retells the tradition of loyalty which Spotted Fawn clung to. "As she had been doing before, Red kept climbing a hill alone each day and from it looked for hours toward the east. For years she maintained the vigil, then finally yielded to Bill Bransford's entreaties . . ."[6] Other sources note that Bransford sought the help of Ceran St. Vrain in his fruitless courtship of Spotted Fawn. Ceran showed Spotted Fawn a certificate purported to be Marcellin's death certificate. Only then, we are told, did she accept Bransford's proposal.

By this time, Spotted Fawn and her children were living at Mora in present northern New Mexico, for ". . . at Marcellin's insistence that she be cared for, Ceran agreed to take her to Mora, where he had just moved from Taos to set up a gristmill and another store" (333). Marcellin had left Fort St. Vrain for good, whether he could admit it or not.

In 1851, Marcellin came to Mora to take his two boys back to Missouri. Unless this was done secretly and away from Spotted Fawn's knowledge as to who actually came for Felix and Charles, it was probably at this point that Spotted Fawn finally came to believe that her marriage to Marcellin St. Vrain was over. Perhaps because of the "death certificate" shown her by Ceran on Bransford's behalf, or the event of her boys going to live with their father and his relatives in Missouri, Spotted Fawn at last agreed to marry William Bransford. She kept her daughter Mary Louise with her.

Bransford had established a ranch east of Trinidad on land given to Ceran St. Vrain's family, a vast tract in northern New Mexico and southern Colorado called the Vigil-St. Vrain Land Grant. Bransford obtained a seat on the County bench and Judge Bransford and his new family settled down. Declaring this a happy ending, Lavender says of Spotted Fawn, "She became a Catholic and bore Bill seven children . . .". And it was a happy outcome: the remainder of her life as a rancher's wife was apparently happy and full. Bransford's energy and persistence in winning Spotted Fawn, whom he called "Red," had sufficient romantic appeal that local historians took its status as a real-life love story for granted. Anonymous note-takers, whose papers are filed in the library at Bent's Fort, need only allude to Bransford's difficult courtship and powerful love story, assuming it to be common knowledge in southeastern Colorado's folk traditions.

Spotted Fawn accompanied her new husband on familiar routes of Bent, St. Vrain Co. business, spending some time in Taos as well as Mora and Trinidad. While at Taos, she posed for a daguerreotype photo and later Francis Cragin made a penned sketch based on the photograph. Thus, the family and other interested persons have a good likeness of this remarkable early citizen of what would become Colorado.

In 1867, on New Year's Eve day, twenty-one year old Mary Louise St Vrain married a Mr. Skelley, about whom very little could be discovered by family genealogists; he apparently died young. According to the family genealogy by Paul Augustus St. Vrain, Marcellin's son by his Missouri white wife, "Mary Louise

St. Vrain . . . married (1st) John Skelley in Mora, New Mexico in 1867." Cragin claims this was 1864: but the more recent genealogical chart prepared by Marcellin's great-grandson, Hyman St. Vrain, shows the Skelley children born after 1867: William Robert on November 15, 1869 and Cora on May 1, 1872. When Mary, after John Skelley's death, married E.B. Sopris in 1889, he adopted the two Skelley children, William Robert and Cora and their surnames were changed to Sopris.

At this point, the testimony of Spotted Fawn's grandson, William Robert Sopris published in the *Colorado Magazine,* by the Colorado State Historical Society, in its March, 1945 edition, is the best public source of information about Spotted Fawn's last two-thirds of her life, the Bransford years. This article, "My Grandmother, Mrs. Marcellin St. Vrain," presents recollections during a time from ages 4 to 8 when W.R. lived with Spotted Fawn on the ranch 15 miles from Trinidad. His mother, Mary Sopris and his stepfather, E.B. were busy helping to raise a large family of "step-brothers, step-nieces and nephews, giving them a home with us." From Grandmother Bransford, W.R. heard his first bed-time stories, learned how to catch trout with his bare hands, and received his first geography lesson: that way is the Santa Fe Trail, that way is Westport, Missouri, that way is Bent's Fort, and that other way is Texas, the place the longhorns we see on cattle drives come from. She called W.R. 'Partner', and in later years the Bransfords moved to Trinidad with Mary Louise. W.R. and Spotted Fawn played casino against grand-father Bill and W.R.'s sister Cora. The loser had to pay up a quarter to "buy the apples." Occasionally Spotted Fawn would cut a few corners to assist their chances of winning the game, but "Grandfather would say, 'Hold on Red, you can't do that.' She would appeal to me, refusing to take his word that what she was doing was not permitted. When we lost, as we frequently did, Mr. Bransford would say, 'Jinks and I won; pay up.' Grandmother would reach her hand into the deep pocket of her dress and bring up the two bits."[7]

This full-blooded Sioux woman's attitude toward Indians is interesting. Her grandson remembers a family drama in which Buffalo Bill Cody came to the ranch, from his station at Fort Lyon, asking her to intercede in a feared uprising; a combined force of Utes, Apaches and Comanches were reported heading north to do battle with the Cheyenne. "Because grandmother had known many Utes during her residence in Taos, and Cheyennes while at Fort St. Vrain and Wyoming, she was sought as an ambassador to go out and meet them. A Ute boy, employed on the ranch, who had been raised by her, was to accompany her. The juncture was made, the invasion vanished. I do not recall how."[8]

W.R. Sopris further explains,

When news of the battle in which General Custer was killed reached her, she worried, kept to herself for days and wept. As the wife of a French-Indian trader she met and knew many Americans, among them General Fremont, Francis Parkman (the historian), William Cody and many others. . . . She realized and saw the hopelessness of the struggle against the whites. Her judgment, if not her sympathy, at that time, while she may have recalled the treaties broken by the whites, must have told her that the end had come in the fight to avoid being taken onto the reservation. She had long mistrusted and disliked Sitting Bull; she expressed no regret that her wild and ungovernable nephew, Crazy Horse, had also been killed (Sopris 67).

Judge Bransford died the day after Christmas, 1881 (perhaps '83, according to Cragin). Spotted Fawn drew into herself after this, became uncommunicative, and according to W.R. Sopris, would "walk to the foothills and remain there most of the day." She herself passed away at the age of 61, on April 12, 1886 in Trinidad, Colorado (Cragin 4:30). Friday the Arapaho had died on the Wind River Reservation in 1883 and Marshall Cook in Johnstown, Colorado in 1884.

The preceding synthesis of Spotted Fawn's life may appear to the reader an irrelevancy for the purposes of this book, which ought to sustain unity around the question of the authenticity of Marshall Cook's account of events at Fort St. Vrain. But these details create a valuable testimony against the common stereotype that French traders had no respect for marriage with an Indian, that those liaisons were never taken seriously but that white mountain men and traders always adopted a "love 'em and leave 'em" attitude, often without taking responsibility for the offspring of these common law marriages or other liaisons. Spotted Fawn's history tells a different story: Marcellin and Ceran St. Vrain saw to her welfare and that of the children. Her loyalty remains as a testimony on Marcellin's behalf, a hint that he was not so heartless, that whatever he had done, it was not to be judged on face value as a massacre of innocents, but something along the lines of a metaphor—as though a small man and lonely man had triumphed over men much larger, those Indians whose cultural mores gave them a license to kill innocent by-standers to achieve vengeance. In those days, when issues of justice arose, vigilante justice was all that was possible. As we have seen, Friday the Arapaho also understood the self-destructiveness of Indians' policy of a never-ending cycle of vengeance.

We would currently have a clearer idea how to evaluate Cook's manuscript if Spotted Fawn had been forthcoming about the events surrounding Marcellin's last days at Fort St. Vrain not long after Mary Louise was born. Not only was Spotted Fawn completely silent on the issue, (and maybe she did not know) but her grandson W.R. apparently had asked her about rumors of his "trouble with the Indians" and gotten no response. He reports, in the 1945 article we have just reviewed, that "Marcellin left for Missouri, after, as the story goes, his accidental killing of an Indian. My only source for that story was General E.B. Sopris (my stepfather)" (Sopris 63). Neither Spotted Fawn nor her direct descendants spoke to the issue but left it to Marcellin's Colorado son-in-law to render an account. Marcellin's son Paul Augustus St. Vrain also published this as a rumor (*Genealogy*, 1943) to explain the event that was otherwise treated reticently as a kind of skeleton in the distinguished family closet.

Marcellin's story: That summer of 1846 at Bent's Fort we hear about Marcellin from Lieutenant J.W. Abers, a topographical engineer who spent the summer season at Bent's Fort recuperating from malaria. Abers was too sick to accompany Kearny and the Army of the West into Mexico as he had intended. From Abers' journal we learn that Marcellin was in charge in the absence of William Bent. According to Susan McGoffin's diary, Kearny's army left Bent's Fort about August 1, 1846. Most of the expatriated Americans then in the Rocky Mountain region joined in the effort in some way. This meant that Spotted Fawn and her children might have been left in the care of the Mexican engagees and Indian helpers while Marcellin filled the shoes of the booshway at Bent's Fort. Or, she may have accompanied Marcellin to Bent's Fort that early summer until the booshway could send her and the children back to Fort St. Vrain. In fact, we do not know what happened to Spotted Fawn except her own testimony that she had met Francis Parkman.

Not long after this, Francis Parkman stopped at Fort St. Vrain, finding the place dilapidated, the gates torn from their hinges, the weeds thick on the placita. He gives the impression in his book *The Oregon Trail* that it had been long and completely deserted, but we know from W.R. Sopris' memoir of his grandmother that Spotted Fawn was acquainted with Parkman. Parkman might have found her there (or at Fort Laramie) and no doubt she knew the routines of making visitors welcome. One imagines he benefited from her vegetable garden at least. But if Parkman found only Indians and Mexicans at Fort St. Vrain, this would have been the same, perhaps, to him as no one at all. They didn't count in the white man's census.

The Mexican War was not a prolonged affair and by late August the campaign had ended. New Mexico became U.S. territory and Charles Bent its first governor. William Bent was back at Bent's Fort and he must have been enraged at the last and most outlandish of Marcellin's escapades. All his patient mediation among Indian groups constantly warring with one another, the carefully built trade relationships with the Indians along the eastern Front Range of the central Rockies were being threatened. Charles Bent, who mediated such company disputes, was nonplused, we must surmise, and Ceran St. Vrain sympathetic to his brother's plight would have had to mediate along with Charles as to what solution might be best.

Much confusion arises because Marcellin did not return to Fort St. Vrain after the fall of 1846 or 1847. What became of him after that was for many years an enigma. In public records Marcellin simply dropped out of sight. Colorado historians had no idea what had become of him until, in 1943 or 1944, Marcellin's son by a later marriage to a white woman named Elizabeth Murphy published a family history. This genealogy was the work of Paul Augustus St. Vrain. In 1952 LeRoy Hafen reported that when the site of Old Fort St. Vrain was dedicated by the DAR in 1911 Marcellin's daughter was present as guest of honor but no one then knew what had become of her father:

> Marcellin St. Vrain, who was usually in charge of the fort, appeared to have dropped out of sight; and what became of him had, to students of the fur trade period, been a mystery. So it was a delightful surprise when Paul A. St. Vrain a son of Marcellin, presented and published his father's story in 1944. Marcellin's sudden disappearance from the West is thus explained by the family. While Marcellin was engaged in a friendly wrestling match with an Indian, the latter suffered an injury from which he died. The Indian's relatives did not look upon the death as accidental, so Marcellin was advised to leave at once for the States. He did so.[9]

Hafen thus followed the family's account, as Paul Augustus St. Vrain heard it, and as William Robert Sopris heard it—and as the Bent, St. Vrain Co. published it in the summer of 1846. Here is the St. Vrain *Genealogy* account:

Paul St. Vrain's "Genealogy of the Family of DeLassus and Saint Vrain," identified the three children of Marcellin and his Sioux wife—Felix, Charles and Mary Louise. Francis

W. Cragin interviewed Mary Louise and Charles in the first decade of the twentieth century. No hint of massacre or atrocity did their memories reveal. In 1943–44, the St. Vrain family genealogy, however, did describe "trouble" between Marcellin and the Indians in his vicinity.

> According to Paul St. Vrain, Marcellin left Fort St. Vrain in 1846 because [he] engaged in a friendly wrestling match with a young Indian brave in which the latter suffered an injury which resulted in his death. It seems the friends of the young Indian did not look upon this as an accident and became so aroused and threatening that Marcellin was advised by his brother Ceran and the Bent brothers to leave the territory. He followed their advice, returning to the home of his father in Missouri.[10]

Thus, David Lavender, writing in 1954, assumes that the wrestling match occurred at Bent's Fort, probably because Marcellin was there in the summer of 1846, and it was from there that the account of Marcellin's "trouble with the Indians" was published. Apparently the Arapaho, who found Fort St. Vrain deserted after the killing of their clansmen, or clansman, as the case may be, followed Marcellin to Bent's Fort and demanded justice. Lavender, referring to them as "yammering Indians" says that "Ceran and William advised him to get out of the country, go back to Missouri" (332) and then in an end note Lavender declares: "The exact date of Marcellin's flight cannot be determined. His granddaughter, Mrs. [sic] W.R. Sopris says the summer of 1848. Paul St.Vrain (Genealogy 24) says either 1847 or 1848. I am inclined to think it was the fall of 1848" (n9. 442). And, as I have said, I believe it was no later than the fall of 1847 since Mary Louise says she was one year old when her father left.

When he did return to Missouri, Francis Cragin testifies, Marcellin spent some time "in a sanitarium and recovered shortly." No one knows quite what this means but he certainly had problems enough to suffer nervous ills. In his 1952 article on Fort St. Vrain, LeRoy Hafen comments that Marcellin had been rumored to have committed suicide. Those who took that claim on faith thought he had died not long after his return to his family estate near St. Louis, so they did not wonder what had become of him after the early 1850's. He may have suffered from a depressive illness, but the one thing quite believable is that Marcellin St. Vrain became temperamentally unsuited for life in a place that Rufus Sage aptly described, in 1839, as "a howling wilderness." Marcellin's return home probably had curative powers of itself. He would live another twenty years, presumably prosperous ones, surrounded by a large family.

This issue, too, was clarified by Paul St. Vrain's genealogy of 1943, as he took up Marcellin's story after his return to Missouri. Marcellin married a white woman and had ten children more, among them Paul Augustus, and in Missouri Marcellin lived out his days. Concerning this stage of his father's life, Paul St. Vrain's *Genealogy* states:

> After this return to Missouri, Marcellin married Elizabeth Jane Murphy, June 26, 1849 at Florissant, Missouri, and soon thereafter moved to Ralls County Missouri, and built the first flour mill in that country. He continued to operate this mill until his death March 4, 1871. He is buried at Salem churchyard, a few miles from the present town of Center, Missouri. Mrs. St. Vrain died December 4, 1880 and is buried . . . at Salem (19–20).

Shortly after his marriage and the establishment of the flour mill near his family estate in Ralls County, Marcellin made one last journey to the West—to retrieve his two sons from Ceran at Mora, in northern New Mexico,and to bring his family back to Missouri. In the event, it was the two boys who returned with him; Spotted Fawn and Mary Louise stayed at Mora.

Paul A. St. Vrain's *Genealogy* surmises:

> This must have been around 1848 or '49, as the second son, Charles, was able in later life to recall incidents of that trip (such as riding at night on horseback in front

of his father, with his brother Felix behind) so he must have been four or five years old at the time. With no positive information at hand, it is presumed that some sort of arrangement was made and agreement reached with his wife, who kept the young daughter, Mary Louise, and that Indian custom with regard to separation and dissolution of the marriage was satisfied, as the Indian wife, Royal, later married William A. Bransford, an assistant to Colonel Ceran St. Vrain.

Since Paul had grown up in the household with his half-brothers Felix and Charles, his testimony is reliable. Then, too, Charles would recall in later life how he helped his father daily at the flour mill. Although Felix died too young to describe those earliest years, Charles, in his interview with Francis Cragin, stated that the year of Marcellin's return to the West was 1851. Therefore, Marcellin retrieved his sons sometime between 1849 and 1851, having had time to heal, resettle and get his business started before taking his sons, who in 1851, would have been nine (Felix) and seven (Charles) to raise in Missouri.

These events caused a rift between the two St. Vrain brothers that never healed. Parkhill Forbes, in his book *The Law Goes West,* reprints Ceran St. Vrain's will, noting that Marcellin is not included, because the brothers had been estranged. Edward Broadhead in his biography of Ceran simply reprints the will without comment. This would have meant severe consequences in that Marcellin's heirs had been excluded from the Vigil-St. Vrain lands. And although Ceran spent very little time at Fort St. Vrain, it would be Ceran memorialized on the DAR monument and not its scapegrace booshway.

None of this brings us closer to understanding who the victims were that the Arapaho killed, allegedly the wife and child of Marcellin. However, Marcellin reportedly had two wives, the second being known around Bent's Fort as Tall Pawnee Woman. O.W. Pratt's recollection dated 1838 is the source for this and for the rumor that Marcellin had two children by this second wife. David Lavender renders an unattractive description of her: "a rawboned Pawnee six feet tall, noted chiefly for her ability to tan buckskin. She was the mother of two boys, but when Marcellin fled she was apparently left to shift for herself and drifted up to Pueblo, where she perhaps married one of the hangers-on and then, either single or wed, scratched out a garden of corn, pumpkins, and melons" (333).

She seems a phantom of Pratt's imagination, (he was notoriously unreliable as a witness) or perhaps of Marcellin's, and when historians name her children, we are disconcertingly faced with a Felix or a Charles—and begin to wonder if Spotted Fawn had a double identity, one as a Sioux (the French word for "enemy") at Fort St. Vrain and another as "Pawnee," those most entrenched, despised enemies of the Arapaho. The only other support for Big/Tall Pawnee Woman's existence is William Bent's son George's comment in a 1913 letter to historian George Hyde that he had once seen Marcellin's Indian wife, Big Pawnee Woman, in Pueblo, Colorado. If these were two different wives and proof of Marcellin's polygamy as Lavender believed, Marcellin certainly had a talent for choosing women who would be an offensive presence to his Arapaho Indian clients. And, if George Bent didn't get the two confused, we have another Indian wife who outlived the events of the summer of 1846 at Fort St. Vrain. It follows that if Cook is literally correct about a wife and child of St. Vrain's being murdered, Marcellin must have had three Indian wives! Not hardly.

The cultural differences between white families and Indian families was so great, that much got lost in translation. For this reason the term "sister" in describing Spotted Fawn's relationship to Red Cloud is placed in quotes, to alert readers that the meaning may not be what white families call "siblings," but rather might mean "of the same clan—even distant cousins." In the same spirit, Marcellin's "wife and papoose" should be interpreted liberally, as persons who were under his protection at Fort St. Vrain. To have ended their lives would have been a great insult to his role as *pater familia* for a large, extended family, "his family," at Fort St. Vrain. Taking revenge, or vigilante justice upon the gang who murdered the

woman and child would have been appropriate as the wrongdoing—"cold-blooded murder"—was sufficient provocation.
The difficulty came when a "cycle of vengeance" began to roll,
and the Indians then demanded revenge for Marcellin's killing
of their brothers and sisters. Had they achieved this, the
whites would have to avenge Marcellin's death—and a never-
ending cycle of violence would be the order of the times. It was
better to end it, and so Marcellin returned to his family estates
and lived out a life that seems to have been satisfactory.

The interpretations of the facts then, might be described as
alternatives. First: Marcellin was polygamous, like many other
French voyageurs of his time, and had two wives, one named
Spotted Fawn at Fort St. Vrain with three known offspring and
one at Bent's Fort named Big Pawnee Woman with two
unknown offspring (this is the conclusion we must draw from
David Lavender's account in *Bent's Fort*). (2) Or, Spotted Fawn
and Big Pawnee Woman were the same, and Marcellin St.
Vrain referred to them in whatever terms meaning "enemy of
the Arapaho" occurred to him.—or meant enemy to his audience as he saw them; (3) Marcellin had put out the story that
the Arapaho killed his wife and child at Fort St. Vrain to justify his attack upon the Indians, and since Spotted Fawn and
Mary Louise were alive and well, and there was no real rationale, he created a phantom wife and papoose to shore up his
account, telling Pratt he had two wives and five children when
in fact he had one Indian wife and three children—these relatives being incontrovertibly existent and testimony about them
handed down in numerous sources. Perhaps none of these is
correct. Public records show only one wife, Spotted Fawn.
Marcellin's alleged polygamy is surrounded with vagueness.

It is, after all, the judgment of this writer that the third
hypothesis is the most likely. Big Pawnee Woman is a phantom
created by Marcellin to distract nosy inquirers into what had
really occurred at Fort St. Vrain. The Indian wife that George
Bent, Jr. saw in southern Colorado could well have been Spotted
Fawn. As to the present inquiry into Cook's account, no matter
how many wives Marcellin had, we are no closer to identifying
the wife and papoose that the Arapaho killed.

In conclusion, then how did the character of Marcellin St.Vrain affect the fate of his adobe trading post? In the wrestling match between the raw wilderness along the old Trapper's Trail and the young Marcellin, clearly the wilderness won. The fort was closed down part time in 1845 and then, closed down altogether in 1847 through 1848. But there was another side to Marcellin's character, one which pleased the explorer John Fremont so much that he put Fort St. Vrain on the map for the remainder of the nineteenth century and into the twentieth. This segment of Fort St. Vrain's history will be examined in the next chapter. It will include an incident in Fremont's journey to demonstrate that the Arapaho were altogether capable of the action which compelled Marshall Cook to include it in his history of early Colorado.

Notes to Chapter Three
The Booshway of Fort St. Vrain

[1]Kristin Ewing Parson, *The Trader on the American Frontier: Myth's Victim,* College Station: Texas A&M UP, 1977.

[2]Paul Augustus St. Vrain, *Geneology of the Family of DeLassus and Saint Vrain,* self-published, Kirksville, MO, 1943, 1–3.

[3]George Hyde, *Letters of George Bent,* 86-7. See also p. 19 for an antelope-hunting diagram as discussed above.

[4]David Lavender believed the trouble occurred at Bent's Fort where a confrontation of angry Arapaho came to protest to Marcellin about a dead relative. He also suggests that Spotted Fawn was and remained at Bent's Fort after Marcellin left the west. However, the event which angered the Arapaho happened, at Fort St. Vrain. Spotted Fawn may have watched for Marcellin's return from the ridges near there. She also probably spent some time with her Sioux relatives to the north. She did recall times at Fort Laramie.

[5]Francis Cragin, *Early West Notebooks* 8:38, transcription at Western History Dept., Denver Public Library, Denver, CO.

[6]David Lavender, *Bent's Fort,* 333

[7]William Robert Sopris, "My Grandmother Mrs. Marcellin St. Vrain, 66; In *Colorado Magazine,* March, 1945, 63–68.

[8]Sopris 65.

[9]LeRoy Hafen, "Fort St. Vrain," *Colorado Magazine,* October, 1952: 29, 4: 251.

[10]Paul A. St.Vrain, 18–19 (item 24).

Cover page, autobiography of John Charles Fremont in which he desribes his western journeys.

IV. The Great Fourth of July Ice Cream Social

If Fort St. Vrain had depended solely on the successes of the company trappers and (white) mountain men, it would have been out of business and gone from the maps shortly after 1840—when European trade with China opened up and silk hats replaced beaver in the world fashion market for men's finery. Those American "border" companies out of St. Louis and northward along the Missouri River which were able to adjust to the new market for buffalo hides, robes, leather and cord (made from the braided mane of the buffalo) remained in business. Bent, St. Vrain Co. was one of these. Not only were its Mexican bases in Taos and Santa Fe not dependent on the beaver fur market alone, but William Bent had established solid relationships with his in-laws the Cheyenne and was a gifted negotiator and mediator with Indian peoples in general. And, when the commerce of the untamed west began to focus on bison products, the Indians became proportionally more important to the white traders. Plains Indian men were skilled buffalo hunters much needed in those earliest days, and the women were crafts persons without peer in the tanning of the buffalo hides for leather and robes. Although this was an advantage for William Bent and the senior company partners, Marcellin St. Vrain did not adjust, it seems, to the diplomatic requirements inherent in these new trade networks, not finding the local Arapaho to his liking, and the majority of his Sioux in-laws remained, for the most part, north around Fort Laramie.

Meanwhile, in the early 1840's, political issues within the Federal government fomented. Already the possibility of a North-South division of the Union manifested itself—a great divorce over slavery was contemplated. The railroad industry was flourishing and U.S. leaders dreamed of transcontinental passage—even as the Senate grappled with a legal paradox because the "public lands" of the Louisiana Purchase were often also the Indian territories guaranteed by the United States government. Citizens with voices in the new democracy argued over liquor laws (dry vs. wet) and the tomfoolery of women's rights and of the advantages of a "Little America" vs. an idea that came by a journalistic accident to be called "Manifest Destiny." Fort St. Vrain played a role in that cause and in the process became the setting for several kinds of stories—some true, i.e., historical, some true-in-a-way (fiction) and some false (lies). The purpose of this section of our history is to sort out some of these different kinds of stories.

During this exciting period of American history, a Virginian named John Charles Fremont led in 1842 and 1843 the most prestigious group of visitors ever to sojourn at Fort St. Vrain. Just the year before, in 1841, he became the husband who had stolen in elopement the hand of Jessie Benton, daughter of the powerful Missouri Senator, Thomas Hart Benton. This was only one of the events in Fremont's life testifying to his incredible luck. He was truly a "child of Destiny." Born into lowly circumstances in Savannah, Georgia, and reared on the fringes of the refined southern culture of Virginia, Fremont acquired during his lifetime a most impressive record of public service and high office. During ten years after his marriage to Jessie Benton in 1841, he assumed the leadership of five exploratory journeys across the continent, traversing more total miles than any other American explorer in the west. He served as U.S. Senator from California (1850–51). He was the new Republican party's first presidential nominee in 1856; he lost the election to Buchanan. He served as a general in the Civil War (1861-1865). Before his death in relative obscurity in New York City in 1890, he served as Arizona's Territorial governor from

1878-1883. In subsequent decades, every student of American history would remember John C. Fremont by the nickname hero-hungry Americans would bestow upon him: "The Pathfinder." He was a powerful representation of the Horatio Alger type of hero—"rags to riches"—that the American public of the late nineteenth century so loved.

In his role as a leader of men, however, Fremont revealed deep character flaws which has earned him severe criticism by American historians. There seem to be two Fremont's— the public, popular hero versus the reality, a cock-of-the-walk—arrogant and foolhardy—but fortunately the central figure of his own published mythology. The incident which brought about an early end to his first expedition of 1842 serves as a good example. Fremont's guide on this trip was none other than the excellent Kit Carson. The group had followed the "Great Platte River Route," across central Nebraska and when they came to a crossing, they found the river had risen alarmingly. Fremont stowed his scientific instruments, which were crucial to the topographical aim of this U.S. Senate-sponsored expedition, into a canoe. In describing the incident, Francis Cragin wrote: "Carson had advised Fremont . . . not to trust his instruments to a precarious canoe in such dangerous waters, but the advice was unheeded and the result that Carson had anticipated came to pass." Fremont and the precious instruments upended midstream. Fremont, who had planned to push on to Oregon Territory the following spring, turned back at Fort St. Vrain, bringing his famous journey to a premature conclusion. We receive a vivid vignette of the relationship between Fremont and his men from Cragin:

> There was some bantering of Fremont by the boys when his instruments got spilled and broken and he himself was fished out of the water by Carson below the N. Platte canon [canyon]. He had wanted them all to jump in and get out his instruments, and to every excited order of the "great pathfinder" Chamberlain and they returned only some laughing reply. His

"sworn in" men from St. Louis however, succeeded in recovering the stuff, part of it badly damaged.[1]

Fremont had exacted an oath of loyalty unto death from these hapless St. Louis men who had been with him from the beginning. In this he was fortunate; furthermore, Fremont's luck consisted not only in having Kit Carson to fish him out of the river, but above all in being the one to write the "Topographical Report" to the U.S. Senate, published March, 1843, whereby he could maximize the environmental dangers and minimize his own folly.

The loss of tools, however—no matter how expensive—hardly compares to the reckless jeopardy of those human lives with which a leader is entrusted, and on Fremont's fourth journey in the west several years later, he plunged into the Sangre de Cristo mountains late in the fall, despite warnings from veteran mountain men, Old Bill Williams and others, that the mountains were treacherous so late in the season. In disregarding this advice, Fremont subjected ten of his men to death by exposure and starvation and barely escaped himself. This was the most egregious of Fremont's follies, but his reputation survived, and we read, typically, the memoir of a Congregational minister written in 1859, W.H. Goode, who was traveling from Omaha to the Pikes Peak Gold Region, as he associated the South Platte valleys with the explorer John Fremont, thinking of him as the trailblazer, and when he published his journal, titled *Outposts of Zion,* he refers to Fremont as "the distinguished mountaineer."[2]

In fairness, we should remember that Fremont himself disclaimed the title, "Pathfinder," as he should have. Early Colorado historian Wilbur Stone, writing in 1916, was among many to counter the tide of popular imagination and comment that Fremont was "in many ways not the first to discover various trails and passes" (Stone I: 56). The same wisdom accounts for Cragin's sarcastic tone in the above quotation and his placing "great pathfinder" within quotes.

The twentieth century biographer Bil Gilbert was so indignant at Fremont's high popular estimation that, in his biography of one of the West's unacknowledged but true trail-blazers, Joseph Walker, he spends several pages discussing Fremont's dubious reputation among frontiersmen of good sense. Gilbert reminds us of Fremont's cartographer Charles Preuss and his constant grumbling in his journal—unpublished in English until 1959—against his employer, calling him a "posturing, lightweight popinjay." Gilbert quotes Walker's acidic conclusion that he would adjudge Fremont "as timid as a woman were it not casting an unmerited reproach on the sex." General Stephen Watts Kearny, commenting on the California "Bear Flag Rebellion" in which Fremont participated, found Fremont "personally exasperating and insubordinate as a junior officer." Gilbert summarizes Fremont's madcap campaign in California: "Without orders and as an active military officer he had entered a foreign country [Mexico's California] and beyond whatever other subversion he may have engaged in, committed what amounted to an act of war." Kearny succeeded in having Fremont court martialled over his conduct in that brief conflict, but the incident did Fremont's reputation no lasting harm; as usual, his luck prevailed over his follies.[3]

Fremont, we may conclude, was a folk hero in the worst sense of "mythic," when the traditional images do not conform to historical realities. The foregoing summary is not mere debunking of Fremont but valid corrections to popular imagination. Fremont has a remarkable record of public service and westward exploration. He was a fine botanist and cartographer. He was not a "pathfinder" or the valiant dashing hero doing battle with marauding Indians, even though his writings suggest so. To admire him for the wrong reasons is an injustice. He often exercised poor judgment in leadership situations, acting rashly or arrogantly. The heightened self-image that resulted from his own written report represents both the worst kind of folk tale and folk hero. We are advised to admire Fremont for the right reasons, based on his genuine achievements rather than blindly following his own bids for admiration based on a false image of himself projected in his writings. It is the former kind of posturing and propagandizing that has given mythology a bad name in some people's minds.

When Fremont was not exaggerating the dangers of his environment, he often maximized the alleged attractions of the wilderness. His future biographer did not lightly subtitle Fremont's life story "Spearhead of Manifest Destiny." Two stories exemplifying this are set along the valleys of the South Platte. The first one I will call "Mint Juleps and Noble Savages." It is a simple story which Fremont placed into his topographical report of 1843 and into his memoirs written later.

In the spring and summer of 1842, during Fremont's first expedition to the west, he followed Stephen Long's trail, eventually called by Matthes the Great Platte River Road. Fremont turned southeastward where the South Platte flows into the North Platte in present southwestern Nebraska. He then followed the South Platte upstream to Fort St. Vrain, a journey of about 200 miles. Approximately midway between these two points, Fremont came upon an island in the South Platte and the home of Baptiste Charbonneau, a mixed blood, whose father was the French voyageur Toussaint and his mother the renowned "Bird Woman," Sacajawea, Lewis and Clark's Shoshone Indian guide. Charbonneau ironically named his island, St. Helena, thinking not only of the exile caused by his divided heritage but that represented by this raw wilderness, so far from the civilized centers of St. Louis and Europe where, at the behest of William Clark, he had received an education. Now, in 1842, he was a trader employed by the Bent, St. Vrain Company. Fremont's party found Charbonneau on his island with his trading cart and supplies, and to their immense delight and overwhelming surprise, he spoke to them in English and offered them hospitality—a genuine Noble Savage with European manners! Charbonneau offered them dollops of his whiskey. This was very likely not much better stuff than the gut-wrenching "Taos Lightning" most of the traders stocked. Mint growing wild on the prairie was available. Fremont, ever the southern gentleman, assured his reading public back East that this Noble Savage served his party "mint juleps." This is the first instance of Fremont's publishing his "myth of gentility" in order to counteract the

This view of Bap Charbonneau's Island of St. Helena, a 200 acre site in the South Platte was taken in 1913 by W.L. Putnam of Orchard, Colorado for the DAR album. 'Looking northwest across the main chanel of the Platte and the upper half of the island. The trees showing dimly at the left extend up the south bank of the river for possibly a mile and a half, and form a part of what is now known as Fremont's Orchard'. The island no longer exists. Courtesy, Greeley Centennial Chapter, DAR.

image, cultivated by Stephen Long, of these prairie lands as a "Great American Desert."

A few days later, Fremont reached Fort St. Vrain (July 9, 1842) and here he met a fellow French aristocrat, Marcellin St. Vrain, the man of impeccable manners and "customary kindness," who rolled out the red carpet for his guests, representatives of the United State Senate, guardians of the Louisiana Purchase. Although Fremont did not stay long, because of the accident with his equipment in the river, and he soon turned back toward St. Louis and Washington, he created Fort St. Vrain as an image in the popular imagination by highlighting it in the *Topographical Report*, March 1843. In this way, Fremont made a temporary home of Old Fort St. Vrain in the July summers of 1842 and of 1843, found himself a place in traditional history books as "The Pathfinder," and a prominent place for Old Fort St. Vrain in the region's history for another half century. The remainder of this chapter is dedicated to an assessment of Fremont's explorations insofar as the history of Fort St. Vrain continued to accrue a folklore with attendant folk tales. out of the Fremont expedition of 1843.

In his autobiography, Fremont recalls that: "about noon on July 4th [1843]we arrived at the fort [St.Vrain}, where Mr. [Marcellin] St. Vrain received us with his customary kindness and invited us to join him in a feast which had been prepared in honor of the day."[3] All the men in his reduced company looked forward to the period of relaxation and celebration the Indians called the whites' "Big Medicine Day."

This celebration at Fort St. Vrain of July 4, 1843, included the firing of a small piece of brass artillery which Fremont had brought with him. One may reasonably suppose, then, that in 1843, a year or two before its booshway left, Fort St. Vrain did not have its own cannon. It would be food, however, not fire-power that journal-keepers recalled. The special menu of that July 4th day caused a small storm of commentary in the journals and diaries of some of those who were there and it is this particular menu which raises questions about history and folklore for this present study. We begin with one of the stories, a story set first at Fort Lupton and then at Fort St. Vrain.

Colorado and Larimer County author and historian, Zethyl Gates has generously contributed this story, pertinent to Fremont's visit to Old Fort St. Vrain in 1843. It is named "Fremont's Hitchhiker," and in her own words:

For all practical purposes the beaver fur trade was dead by 1843. Trapping beaver had become a thing of the past; even the mountain rendezvous was only a memory. Hard pressed for a reason to stay in the Rocky Mountain country—and make it pay—the traders looked for a new source of income, and found it in buffalo robes and other products from the bison. This was where the money was. The Plains Indians were eager to continue trading for the white man's goods, and steamboat and freight wagon transportation made it easier to ship the heavy hides to eastern markets.

Large fur companies continued to operate out of established trading posts, or "forts," while independent trapper-traders constructed smaller outposts in an attempt to grab a share of the profits. The Trappers' Trail along the eastern base of the Rockies attracted opportunists who found the land along the South Platte River an ideal location on which to build. This area was squarely in the middle of the buffalo range, and where there were buffalo there would be Indians. Almost simultaneously, four fur forts were built nearly within sight of each other: Fort Vasquez, Fort Lupton, Fort Jackson, and Fort St. Vrain. They were small but annoying competition for the larger posts at Fort Laramie to the north and Bent's Fort. to the south, as well as for each other.

There was a certain amount of rivalry even between the smaller forts, yet their occupants enjoyed a camaraderie typical of the fur fraternities of the West. This was due, partly, to the fact that many of the men there were married (common law style) to Indian women. Such an arrangement was a "plus" in Indian country. It more or less guaranteed to the white trader protection (at least from his in-laws' tribe) as well as buffalo hides. Free trappers visited between the forts; military forces were entertained with what luxuries the fort could provide; travelers wrote down their impressions of life there; friendly Indians were invited in on special occasions. Yes—always there were the Indians, sometimes camped in villages outside the fort's protective walls, sometimes just passing by on their way to new hunting grounds.

Such a place was Fort Lancaster, also known as Lupton's Fort—and finally, Fort Lupton. By 1836 Lancaster Lupton had built his post along the South Platte, and had constructed, by 1838, a second trading post, Fort Platte, a short distance north of Fort Laramie on the Laramie River. Disenchanted with army life (he had been a lieutenant in the Dragoons), Lupton found the life of a trader more to his liking. It is not surprising that he took an Indian woman as his wife. Thomass, who gave Lupton several children, took great pride in gardening; the produce she raised delighted the eyes and tastes of travelers who stopped there.

John Fremont did not stop at Fort Lupton on this particular journey but with thirteen men went on to Fort St. Vrain.

(The remainder of his troops, 24 men, had been sent to Fort Laramie, under the command of Thomas Fitzpatrick.) About noon he reached the fort, was welcomed by the manager, Marcellin St. Vrain, and invited to partake in a feast which had been prepared for their arrival. The holiday was thus celebrated in "barbaric luxury" with a feast of buffalo meat, macaroni, and fruit cake said to have been made by Jessie Fremont's niece. There was also ice cream made from snow on Long's Peak. The American flag was hoisted, and a booming salute was fired from the howitzer Fremont had managed to bring along. No wonder the Indians inquired if the American's "Big Medicine Days" came often!

The fourth of July was also celebrated at Fort Lupton but with less restraint. It was common knowledge that Lupton kept a good supply of Taos Lightning on hand, and some of the employees from the neighboring forts had come to join the festivities there. Among them was Thomas Fallon who had until recently been an orderly sergeant in Colonel Charles Warfield's command when that military outfit visited Fort St. Vrain in February of that year. The celebration soon got out of control as the men unloosed their pent-up emotions in a scene reminiscent of the frenzied activities of the old rendezvous.

What started out as a frolic became a disaster. In a savage outburst, Fallon shot one of Lupton's employees, Baptiste Xervier. The bullet entered his back about two inches below the heart, severely fracturing the vertebrae and nearly severing the spinal marrow, according to Rufus Sage who witnessed the Frenchman's death a week later. During that week Xervier suffered more than the agonies of death. He was paralyzed below the waist and repeatedly begged his comrades to "put an end to his miseries." Sage reported that Fallon was allowed to go, and in a few weeks joined Captain Fremont's expeditionary forces to Oregon. No mention was made of the location of Xervier's grave, but it is presumed he was buried near the fort.

The story does not end with Xervier's death, however. Xervier also had an Indian wife, Sally, who was the mother of his two children. They had all lived at Lupton's Fort. What was to become of them, now that the husband and father was dead?

76

Sally was a Shoshone Indian, the daughter of Komoostz, a chief of the tribe. She was born about 1808 in the land of Shoshone near the headwaters of the Green River (Wyoming). When she was quite young, Sally was out hunting berries in the Black Hills with some of her people. Suddenly a party of hostile Sioux Indians surprised the group, and Sally was shot in the neck. The wound was not fatal, and she was cared for by an aunt until she was almost twelve years old.

About this time a wealthy merchant was attracted to Sally as he passed through the country. He took her to St. Louis, Missouri to be educated. For four difficult years Sally stayed there, eventually giving in to her inner longing to rejoin her own people. She ran away. Even the mighty Missouri River did not stop her. She swam across, resting for awhile on an island in the middle of the river before resuming her journey. Somewhere along the trail on the other side Sally stopped at a trapper's log hut to ask for food. Here she met the Frenchman, Baptiste Xervier. After a few weeks of courtship, they were married.

In 1838 the couple was living at Fort Laramie, where Sally gave birth to a daughter, Adelaide. Later a boy was born to them. Baptiste then moved his family to Lupton's Fort, where he was killed. There is a story that before Xervier died, his friend Seth Ward, then the head trader at Fort St. Vrain, promised to take care of Sally and the children. But, now that Baptiste was gone, Sally once again longed to go home to her people.

On or about July 22, Captain Fremont stopped at Lupton's Fort on his return from a brief trip which had taken him south from St. Vrain's Fort to the Arkansas River. He now was accompanied by Kit Carson, who had helped him procure supplies and fresh draft animals from Bent's Fort. Carson agreed to join Fremont as a guide and hunter, as he had done the previous year. Now Sally saw her chance. She told her story to Fremont, and begged to be allowed to go with his party to her homeland. Something about the tragedy struck a sympathetic chord in Fremont's heart. Perhaps he was thinking of his own wife, Jessie Benton Fremont, and wondered if such a thing should happen to her whether someone would help. He agreed to take Sally and her children with him. That is how Sally Xervier and her children became Fremont's hitchhikers.

Fremont recalled the incident and in his *Report of the Exploring Expedition to the Rocky Mountains* (Washington, July, 1845), *he wrote:*

> A French engage, at Lupton's had been shot in the back on the 4th of July, and died during our absence to the Arkansas. The wife of the murdered man, an Indian woman of the Snake nation, desirous, like Naomi of old to return to her people, requested and obtained permission to travel with my party to the neighborhood of Bear river, where she expected to meet with some of their villages. Happier than the Jewish widow, she carried with her two children, pretty little half-breeds, who added much to the liveliness of the camp. Her baggage was carried on five or six pack horses; and I gave her a small tent, for which I no longer had any use, as I had procured a lodge at the fort.

Sally found her people in the vicinity of Fort Bridger, and there she married Barney Ward and reared a second family. While serving as interpreter and teacher among the settlers, she met her brother, called "Indian John" by the pioneers.

Frequently Sally would leave her home in the white community to visit her people in the Shoshone village. The time came, however, when she went away and was never seen again. Like her French husband, Baptiste Xervier, Sally lies somewhere in a lonely forgotten, unmarked grave. Their story and the interlude at Lupton's Fort now belong to history.

Fremont's Shoshone hitchhikers arrived safely at Fort Laramie, but not without incident. About halfway between Fort St. Vrain and Fort Laramie, the group encountered a band of Arapaho warriors who threatened to kill the Shoshone woman and her child because they were members of an enemy tribe. Fremont or one of his lieutenants intervened and the widow and child were protected from harm, perhaps because Fremont represented them as under the protection of the St. Vrain family. The woman Sally lived a long life and her descendant, Noreen Rawlings, told the story as it had been preserved in her family to Zethyl Gates.[4]

Many of the witnesses to the Xervier shooting left written accounts: Rufus Sage, employed at Lupton's Fort, recalled the incident as did Theodore Talbot, who was at Fort St. Vrain with the Fremont expedition. Noting the persons included in Fremont's party as they left Fort St. Vrain on July 26th, Talbot remarks, ". . . also a Snake [Shoshone] woman, the widow of Xervier, with her children, returning to her nation" (28). He also tells us that the man who shot Xervier, Thomas Fallon, formerly an employee at Fort St. Vrain, joined Fremont's expedition in the capacity of Voyageur. Thus, a mass of corroboration allows us to accept Noreen Rawlings' account to Zethyl Gates as historical fact.

An interesting observation in Talbot's journal, however, is his entry of Sunday, July 15, when he notes, "Friday, the starved little hero of the Cimarron, came to bid us good bye, as he accompanies the war party against the Youta [Utah— i.e., Utes and their relatives, the Shoshone and Bannock], now just about leaving. . . ." (24). At this time, more than ten years after Fitzpatrick had found the starving "little hero," Friday would have been about seventeen. He would have been among the group of Arapahoes who, on their way to eastern Utah, threatened Xervier's widow and daughter. And, he may have played a role in preventing their murders, although none of the sources make this claim. Other Shoshone Indians in the vicinity were not so fortunate, as we learn from Fremont's sarcastic cartographer, Charles Preuss.

Preuss' journal entry for August 10, 1843, refers to Xervier's daughter and the threat to the dead man's Indian widow: "I often get pleasure out of the bawling of the Indian child. She is about as old as my little girl, but otherwise, thank goodness, no similarity. The Sioux and Arapahoes have massacred 5 Snake women, caught one boy and later killed him, too. Those noble Indians! One of the Arapahoes had a great desire to scalp our lady" (84).[5]

So, here it is: a real-life account of happenings prior to Marcellin St. Vrain's "revenge" but exactly describing his motive, as the Arapaho demonstrate the policy of killing a woman and child "merely because they belonged to an enemy tribe." If Marshall Cook's "rather fantastic" account is not related to this incident witnessed by Fremont's 1843 explorers, there is no known historical basis for it. It is, sufficient, however, that this example demonstrates the principle at the heart of Cook's account. It provides corroboration, circumstantial evidence, for Friday's memoir and proves Cook's point that by adhering to policies of relentless cycle of vengeance the Indians incurred the enmity of the white immigrants who justified with it their own destruction of the indigenous culture. Thus, it is probable that this event—the massacre of the Snake women and the boy—symbolized for Friday the kind of incident that brought white retribution upon the Indians and resulted in their removal to reservations far from their native hunting grounds, the real occasion for his display of grief at Fort St. Vrain. If Friday's story, told to Marshall Cook in the 1860's (but necessarily referring to the mid-1840's when the St. Vrain's managed the South Platte trading post) was based on another and very similar incident at the fort itself, we cannot know. What is clear is that, given the Arapaho attitude toward ritual and traditional warfare, with "kill 'em quick" (i.e. mercifully, in this case) policies against females and children of the enemy tribe, there is a core of truth in Cook's understanding of Friday's narrative. If the slaying of St. Vrain's wife and child at Fort St. Vrain was not "what really happened,"—to quote the philosopher Aristotle's definition of history—it was "what probably would have happened."

There are two other features of Cook's account, however, which lend support to the supposition that the event Friday described occurred while the Fremont party was on the way from Fort St. Vrain to Fort Laramie in 1843. This is so because folklore dynamics such as "displacements" often occur in oral accounts like the one Friday the Arapaho rendered to Marshall Cook. Cook writes that the cannon went everywhere with "the daring Frenchman." Charles Preuss, using almost the same words, had written in his journal words to the effect that the Frenchman [Fremont] had to drag that cursed cannon everywhere with him. Preuss is referring to the howitzer that Fremont brought on the 1843 journey, the one the War Department vociferously objected to. Preuss considered this additional proof that his employer was a complete ass. But Marshall Cook, writing almost forty years later, takes for granted the militarization, the military presence and practices, of the American West and of course he does not examine his assumptions in a critical way in order to discover anachronisms in them. Assumptions are, by definition, concepts we don't examine critically as a rule.

The second feature concerns the size of 'the Frenchman's' contingency. Cook says St. Vrain had seventy-five men. Marcellin had a maximum of 30 at Fort St. Vrain at any one time. Fremont had 39 when he started from Missouri. Both together had 75, at most, in that mid-summer of 1843. Fremont hired some of Marcellin's men at Fort St. Vrain and probably some of the regular fort employees accompanied Fremont for a day or so toward Fort Laramie, an escort, as it were. Fremont's visit was the excitement of the year, after all. Making allowances for Friday's possible over-estimation of the size of Fremont's group, we still find the number 75 better descriptive of Fremont's company of men than of "St. Vrain's men," and the ambience of military concept in Cook's account applies to the Fremont expedition rather than Marcellin St. Vrain's status at the fur trade post.

Three factors in Cook's account "fit" with historical accounts of Fremont's second expedition in 1843: 1) his departure from Fort St. Vrain with about 75 men; 2) a daring Frenchman who drags a cannon everywhere with him; and 3) Friday's eye-witnessing the terrible Arapaho murders of a Shoshone woman (or women) and her child merely because they were members of an enemy tribe. One supposes, then, a pattern exists in Cook's account whereby certain of the Fremont party's experiences are displaced when that Frenchman—or American of French extraction—is confused and conflated with another Franco-American, Marcellin St. Vrain.

This may explain only the first half of Friday's tale, however, or Cook's, or both, as the case may be. The massacre of Arapaho at Fort St. Vrain was said to be an outcome of these events, and if my surmise is correct, the motivating events did not happen at Fort St. Vrain but *did occur* nearby under Fremont's command and on the prairie route toward Fort Laramie. If the crux of Cook's story is literally true, then Marcellin St. Vrain beguiled the Arapaho with his invitation to an elk barbecue and slaughtered an unspecified number of them using a cannon, perhaps, but more likely with battery guns that were a precursor of the Gatling. Corroboration exists to support the idea that some atrocity involving Marcellin and the Arapaho indeed occurred. But these events are documented as "trouble with the Indians" apparently in the spring of 1846, shortly after his daughter Mary Louise was born. Retribution for the Shoshone woman and papoose seemingly took Marcellin a long time—over two years— in the planning. Perhaps communication really was slow.

I suspect that the two events—the Arapaho killing of the Shoshone women and child near Fremont's camp and Marcellin's firing on the Arapaho were not connected as cause-effect nor was Marcellin's action a crime of passion or revenge. But it is likely that Marcellin planted the connection in Friday's memory when, after the fact and at Bent's Fort the "yammering" Indians demanded restitution for their dead and Friday had to interpret and mediate once again. Marcellin probably used the incident with the Shoshone in a "what goes around comes around" argument. Why should the Arapaho make a big issue of their own dead comrades when they cared nothing for the lives of those unfortunate Shoshone? What Marcellin did to the Arapaho was nothing more than what the Arapaho routinely did to their "enemies." This logic formed the basis of Friday's understanding of a connection between the two incidents and that is what he told Marshall Cook. Today, as we realize that Friday's Arapaho were being sent to a reservation in Wyoming which belonged to the Shoshone we grasp more deeply than ever the enormously cruel ironies of history as well as the reasons for Friday's great sorrow.

In the final analysis, it seems that Marcellin's account of his killing an Indian in a wrestling match is not an adequate explanation of his trouble with the Indians. Cook's finding of a mass grave in 1880 or a bit earlier convinced him of the propriety of connections between Friday's story and his own experience. He could testify to *this* interpretation of Friday's account. In addition, it seems as though Marcellin St. Vrain about 1846 was responsible for killing or ordering the killing of Indians at Fort St. Vrain. His behavior at Bent's Fort at the end of that summer is consistent with that of someone undergoing a nervous breakdown (and his "fleeing the country" as David Lavender puts it), eventually to spend time in a Missouri sanitarium. Even Bil Gilbert's quoting Joseph Walker to the effect that Marcellin quit the hunting trip because he couldn't abide the sandflies sounds like a page out of ancient Greek Aeschylean drama, only here the sandflies are the Furies representing Marcellin guilt to extremes of near madness. David Lavender's benign picture of Marcellin, the exuberant youth who loves hunting and all other sorts of fun and hell-raising, belongs to the early era of Marcellin St. Vrain's western career. Marcellin St. Vrain justified a massacre by referring to wrongs those Indians had done in killing innocents that were enemies. The utter embarrassment is, of course, that Marcellin himself approved of uncivilized levels of conduct and proved that whites were not superior to the Indians. No wonder the whites wanted to forget the story of what really happened at Fort St. Vrain! And no wonder, when the story was finally told by Cook, it had taken a shape that did not challenge the assumptions of white cultural supremacy.

From these grim reflections, we turn to another aspect of that fourth of July at Fort St. Vrain in 1843, which is, for the most part, historical fact, corroborated in other sources in addition to Fremont's own account: the feast. The variations in these, however, are worth comment, since they tell us something about the use of stories presented by those earliest white inhabitants and visitors in northeastern Colorado.

While the firing off of Fremont's howitzer was especially memorable, so, too, was the menu! It consisted of buffalo steaks, macaroni, fruitcake and even ice cream. Macaroni had long been a delicacy, imported from Italy. As the line in the Revlutionary War song says, 'Yankee Doodle stuck a feather in his hat and called it macaroni.' He thus achieved a height of elegance and fashion.[6]

This list has come down to modern historians primarily through LeRoy Hafen's account which he published in his 1952 essay on Fort St. Vrain in *Colorado Magazine.* In turn, Hafen's source was a newspaper account in the *Rocky Mountain Herald,* recalling the information Will Ferrill had gotten from an interview with Colorado's first Territorial governor, William Gilpin. Ferrill's interview was conducted in 1913, sixty years after the 4th of July party at Fort St. Vrain and by then Gilpin was getting old, so it is forgivable if the story wasn't quite right. By the time Hafen reprinted the account, more than a hundred years stood between the narrator and the event. But if we are interested in history as actual happenings, we must wonder how many eyebrows were raised in disbelief when Gilpin reminisced about the good old days of the 1840's. Ice cream? In the sweltering July heat?

Well, maybe. Here is how Hafen reported the festivities:

On his second western expedition Fremont spent July 4, 1843 at Fort St. Vrain. With him was William Gilpin, later to become the first governor of Colorado. Gilpin subsequently told of their celebration of Independence Day. They raised the flag, fired a salute from Fremont's howitzer, and served cake and ice cream. The fruit cake had been made by Senator Benton's niece at St. Louis, milk came from the goats at the fort, and snow for the freezing from Long's Peak.[7]

Ever after, Denver and regional newspapers would use this remarkable narrative of Colorado's "first ice cream social" as interesting filler.

Typically, those early travelers along the South Platte, unaware that Long's Peak raised over 14,000 feet above sea level, misjudged its distance from the river. Fremont claimed that it was 17 miles west. In reality, it is 40; in those days it would have taken four days on horseback for the round trip from the fort to the base of the peak. Another two days would have been requred to reach the summit and return. Even snow from what Gilpin said was the "axis of the universe," the Rocky Mountains, would not have lasted long enough and been cold enough to make ice cream in July. The only way this claim can be brought into any sort of credbility is to suppose that Fort St. Vrain, like Bent's Fort, had an ice house in the river bottom. Ice at Bent's Fort, stored in the Arkansas River in this way, lasted, it is said, into August.

However, the key to the story, as always, lies in the character of the narrator. Unlike Fremont, Gilpin had been born chomping the "silver spoon." He did not have to wait until adulthood and blind luck favored him. He had studied law at the University of Pennsylvania, been appointed to West Point by Andrew Jackson, served in the Missouri legislature, been an advisor to Thomas Hart Benton—and under Van Buren's administration, was the brother of the U.S. Attorney General. Gilpin numbered among President Lincoln's personal bodyguards. He was a visionary, among the first to insist that the Oregon Trail through the South Pass would become a main route for a transcontinental railroad. He was also a Romantic; his descriptions of the West inspired photographers like W. Jackson and promoted a whole new visual style. But not all historians appreciate Romantics. The recent western writer Wallace Stegner said that Gilpin was enthralled by "the castles words can build." Robert Perkin, William Byers' biographer, called him "leather-lunged" and jewel-tongued. Gilpin's descriptions of the South Platte country, in defiance of Stephen Long's 1820 summary, the "Great American Desert," gave railroad land agents their basic script for the next hundred years: The West's climate was imcomparably salubrious, its soils so fertile the farmer didn't even need a plow, etc. Gilpin published one thesis comparing the Rocky Mountains to the mountains of the Holy Land, whence came the Ten Commandments and the wisdom of Jesus. Truly in this view, Fort St. Vrain helped inspire "frontier Zionism." No wonder Colorado pioneer William Byers, accused of being a "visionary" himself, considered Gilpin "a very peculiar man," or that western historian Bernard de Voto believed Gilpin's rhetoric "is and always was nonsense."

Another recollection of that celebration exists: the account of Francis Cragin who tells the story in this fashion:

> On the fourth of July it being a holiday some celebration being planned by the people of the fort, it was understood in the morning between Sergeant Pat White in charge of the stock, and the guard, that Blue and 2 others should stay out with the herd in the forenoon and should be relieved at noon by the sending out of 3 other men; so that all could see something of cannon-firing and other doings and get a chance at the 4th of July dinner which included bread and coffee, by no means every day items of the mountaineers bill of fare. When noon arrived, however, the sergeant came out half drunk with one man to relieve the man of the Fremont party, but told the men of the guard from Taos that they would have to stay out till sundown. Hungry and thirsty from their stay in the hot sun, this proposed treatment was a little more than the mountaineers could stand. They both refused to stay out any longer, and the blustering Pat told them they'd have to and said he'd take none of their back talk. Blue's companion was a meek and timorous French Canadian who was afraid to make further resistance. But Blue invited Pat to make them stay and when he udertook it the swelled up sergeant was soon placed hors du combat or, as Wiggins expresses it, fixed "so that he swelled up in another place, his eyes

being for several days after of the 'goggle' variety . . ." [Kit] Carson, seeing that something was wrong came out and met them and was told all about it. He, telling Fremont, the latter said if ordered to stay out the men should have staid. But Carson stood up for his men's rights though the relations between Fremont and Carson were strained to the point of breaking by the question of right in the matter, [until] the affair was at last allowed to blow over (Cragin XXV: 95–98).

Although the delicacies mentioned here are bread and coffee, not fruitcake and ice cream, the caste system at the early trading forts was quite rigid and the officers' mess would have maintained the usual VIP exclusions with respect to the middle and lower class celebrants. White, Blue and Red would not have been offered the very best fare. It is, therefore, possible that the dinner guests of Marcellin St. Vrain at the "captain's table" had cake and ice cream. But Gilpin did not know that firsthand. When we read Gilpin's biography by Thomas Karnes, we learn that he had followed Fremont's guide Thomas Fitzpatrick to Fort Laramie in mid-June, as Fremont divided his command on June 16th and with a small party hastened to Fort St. Vrain while Fitzpatrick led the others—twenty or so, including Gilpin—to Fort Laramie and from there south to Fort St. Vrain, which they reached on the 16th of July. So Gilpin was not at Fort St. Vrain for that 4th of July celebration he described so vividly in his interview with Will Ferrill in 1913.

Gilpin had probably heard about the great 4th of July ice cream social from Fremont, who as we saw in the episode with Charbonneau the previous year, filtered experiences through the lenses of southern gentility. Bil Gilbert once referred to Gilpin as "a booming bass in the manifest destiny choir." Surely, Fremont provided a solid tenor. These two were not historians, it is true, and the bare facts did not always merit their steadfast attention. We should recall, however, comments such as Rufus Sage's judgement in 1838 that the South Platte valley was "a howling wilderness," and

Long's 1820 description of the area as a desert. When we contrast those facts of the times with the fictions of gentility put
forth by Fremont and Gilpin, we have to admit that flourishing contemporary life along the South Platte proves the latter—not the former—were the true prophets. And prophecy,
especially of the self-fulfilling type, is one of the things good
fictions are for.

Notes to Chapter Four
The Great Fouth of July Ice Cream Social

[1]Francis W. Cragin, "Early West Notebooks," 25:91-92.

[2]W.H. Goode, *The Outposts of Zion,* Cincinnati: Poe and Hitchcock, 1864, 153.

[3]Bil Gilbert, *Westering Man,* New York: Atheneum, 1983, 215.

[4]Zethyl Gates, "Fremont's Hitchhiker." Unpublished manuscript. Loveland, Colorado, September, 2000. Based on accounts in Rufus Sage, *Rocky Mountain Life,* in Charles Preuss, *Exploring With Fremont,* on Fremont's *Memoirs* and reports to the U.S. Senate. Charles Preuss' *Exploring With Fremont* remained for the most part untraslated into English until 1959 and was thus unavailable to our general reading public before.

[5]John Charles Fremont, *Memoirs of My Life—John Charles Fremont,* Belford, Clark & Co., Ca. 1896, 175.

[6]Oral interview with Leon Burlieu, Platterville, CO, December, 2000. Leon Burlieu is a living history French Voyageur at Fort Vasquez and has volunteered in hundreds of school programs about the history of the fur trade in the 1830's of the American West.

[7]LeRoy Hafen, "Fort St. Vrain," *Colorado Magazine,* October, 1952, 245.

Indian Agent Thomas Twiss planned to move his headquarters to Fort St. Vrain in 1856 but his plans changed and he went to Deer Creek in Wyoming.

V. Indian Agency on the South Platte

Upon his return to Washington in 1844, Fremont discussed many issues about the West with Senator Benton, among these: "the Indian problem." Out of these discussions emerged a plan to establish an Indian agency along the eastern base of the Rocky Mountains. It was to be named the Upper Platte and Arkansas Agency. There were, of course, bureaucratic models already in existence, such as the Upper Missouri Agency headquartered at Fort Pierre in present South Dakota. This new agency was needed to license and regulate traders, monitor the Mexican import liquor trade (expressly illegal in dealings with Indians), protect emigrants, keep order among whites, Mexicans and Indians—in general to safeguard all the frontier stakeholders from one another.

Now, we normally think of an Indian agency as a physical structure, probably made of logs, stockade style, where the Agent and his family, if he has one, live and to which the Indians may come to collect annuity goods, shop at a next-door trading post, report problems, hold councils, and establish a kind of "law and order" based on signed treaties, agreements with the United States government, administered through the Senate as funding and treaty-making body—this administration to work closely with that of the War Department, or—a bit later—the Bureau of Indian Affairs within the Department of the Interior.

And although this picture is generally adequate, we do not quite know how one would fit into this neat picture the existence of an Indian agency without a resident agent. However, *Fort St. Vrain was just such an anomaly*. In a twelve year period, between 1846 and 1858, before immigrants "stampeded" into the South Platte valleys in Colorado's Gold Rush era, Fort St. Vrain was used as an *ex tempore* agency convenient to the Arapaho and Northern Cheyenne Indian nations within the vast Upper Platte and Arkansas Agency. There was never, so far as I know, payment to Bent, St. Vrain Co. or to William Bent for such a use of Fort St. Vrain. Perhaps payments were subsumed under monies given to Bent's Fort, the New Bent's Fort, where the first agent, Thomas Fitzpatrick, headquartered and administered his enormous burden of responsibilities.

Fitzpatrick, the same one who had found and adopted the boy Friday the Arapaho, was long a friend to William Bent and all the mountaineers of the previous decade, esteemed by all, He had been the chief guide of Fremont's second expedition to the West.[1] Fremont, who typically carried those he admired with him on his rise to great heights of success and power, recommended Fitzpatrick for the post. Indeed, the U.S. government was fortunate to have such a capable man willing to undertake the task. The Upper Platte and Arkansas Agency encompassed the country between the Arkansas and North Platte rivers in Nebraska and Wyoming, including the eastern foot of the Rocky Mountains from present southern and all eastern Colorado to central Wyoming and parts of western Kansas. His territory and his assignment were immensely challenging.

On August 3, 1846, Fitzpatrick's nomination as Agent of the new Upper Platte and Arkansas Agency, was confirmed by the U.S. Senate. The recommendation which preceded this came from Senator Thomas Hart Benton, who had been briefed by Fremont and others on those expeditions, and was directed to the War Department, Bureau of Indian Affairs. Benton wrote:

> *C Street*   *August 27, 1846*
>
> *Sir,*
>
> *The commission and instructions to Thomas Fitzpatrick, Esq. U.S.I.A. for the Upper Platte and*

Arkansas may be directed to Col. Robert Campbell, merchant, St. Louis, who is himself one of the most reliable men, and one of the best acquainted with Indian affairs, and one of the most efficient friends of the administration in the state of Missouri.

The journal and map of Capt. Fremont will show the locality of the agency, as well as the fitness of Mr. Fitzpatrick for the place, and the particular necessity for an experienced & reliable agent in that quarter.

All the waters of the Great Platte, the Arkansas, and of the Kansas (which lies between them,) will be in his district, but his special duties will be along the base of the mountains which is the great thoroughfare for Indians and white people, for trade, war, hunting, and intercourse with Mexico. Bent's Fort on the Arkansas, St. Vrain's fort on the South Fork of the Great Platte, and Fort Laramie on the North Fork, are the three great positions in this range of country, and the former of the three, as nearest to Mexico, might be made the principal station of the agent, who should not be entirely stationary but traverse his district.

Under the head of Fort Laramie Capt. Fremont shows the mischief done by spirits brought in from Mexico, and gives other reviews of Indian affairs worthy of attention. He has also, by letters on file in the war department, urged the establishment of this agency, and the appointment of Mr. Fitzpatrick. For the rest, his general instructions would be the same as those to the agent on the Upper Missouri.

Yours respectfully,

Thomas H Benton

Fort St. Vrain, recognized by the federal government as one of three main locations in the eastern plains of the Rockies, was included in the Upper Platte and Arkansas Indian Agency, and Thomas Fitzpatrick, who had sojourned there innumerable times before, continued to stop there as it became for the next ten years, the focus of American relations

Senator Benton: 'Bent's Fort on the Arkansas, St. Vrain's Fort on the South Fork of the great Platte, and Fort Laramie on the North Fork are the three great positions in this range of country'. Records of the Upper Platte and Arkansas Agency, Rocky Mountain National Archives, Denver, Colorado.

with the Arapaho and Northern Cheyenne tribes. The Southern Cheyenne continued to gravitate around Bent's Fort just as the various Sioux groups recognized Fort Laramie as a major crossroad for trade and politics.

Although his career was destined to be cut short by illness and death in 1853-54, Fitzpatrick achieved his major goal, treaties with the Indian tribes of the central eastern plains. In 1851, the "Grand Council" of 10,000 Indians gathered near Fort Laramie.to approve the Fort Laramie Treaty. Because Fort Laramie could not accommodate such vast numbers of Indians, the proceedings were removed to Horse Creek, near present Cheyenne, Wyoming. The treaty stipulated the following: safe passage for emigrants, especially numerous on the Oregon Trail, lured by California gold and fertile farmlands. It granted lands between the Arkansas and North Platte rivers to the Sioux, Cheyenne and Arapaho. It authorized the U.S. government to establish military posts on Indian land and to build roads. In addition, an annuity of $18,000 was guaranteed for 50 years. The United State Senate soon amended the treaty, reducing the annuity pay period from 50 years to 15.

Fitzpatrick was compelled to visit the tribes, which were widely scattered. At Fort St. Vrain, the Arapaho and Northern Cheyenne agreed to the new terms. Not long afterward, he left for Washington to deliver personally a report, leaving Mr. Ketchum in charge during his prolonged absence. In his written instructions, Fitzpatrick advises Ketchum to overlook the fact that the traders are not licensed, to treat them as though they were "to avoid trouble." This is the first official acknowledgement that there might be trouble brewing between the traders along the North and South Platte Rivers, and the Indian agents, but it is an important clue to understanding subsequent events leading to Indian wars against the whites.

For the next several years the Cheyenne camped along the South Platte. George Bird Grinnell, writing in 1923, tells of the shooting of White Horse, whose band was camped at Fort St. Vrain in 1854. The general topic of what constituted

95

punishable offenses and what did not provided the focus for this chapter. White Horse had stolen Walking Coyote's wife, and so he and a friend sought recompense, riding twenty miles downstream, from near the site of present Greeley, to White Horse's camp:

> Walking Coyote rode into the fort [St. Vrain] and saw White Horse and his wife—not the woman who had been stolen—sitting on a bench in the hall of the fort. When the two saw Walking Coyote, they arose and walked toward the hands' messroom, and Walking Coyote jumped off his horse and shot White Horse . . . killing him at once. Then Walking Coyote and War Bonnet led their horses outside the gate of the fort and sat down there, and Walking Coyote said, "If anyone has anything to say to me, I am here" (Grinnell, I: 350 1).

No one called Walking Coyote to account. After a short while, Little Wolf, a cousin of the powerful leader, Yellow Wolf, came out and advised the two to return to their camp. Apparently shooting a man who has stolen your wife was not a punishable offense.

Fort St. Vrain was the delivery point for a third of the annuity goods stipulated in the 1851 treaty. Fitzpatrick's close friend and former partner in the Rocky Mountain Fur Company, Robert Campbell, organized the purchase and transportation of these goods from his St. Louis mercantile. After Fitzpatrick's death in early 1854, John.W. Whitfield was named agent of the Upper Platte and Arkansas Agency. Major Whitfield (all Indian agents seem to have carried this title as honorary) also found the assignment of such a vast land and so many various Indian groups arduous. By 1853, a separate treaty with the Kiowa, Comanche and Apache had been negotiated to safeguard the Santa Fe Trail. Now, many additional goods were required to satisfy a second agreement. Unless these shipments of annuities were carefully guarded, they would go "astray", be pillaged at some fort, military or otherwise, between St. Louis and the Rockies—or be lost bit by bit, along the difficult trails.

On the east coast, J.W. Whitfield's first assignment was to procure annuity goods. At Callender, Rogers, and Hilton, "Importers and Dealers in Foreign & Domestic Hardware and Cutlery," of 42 & 44 Pearl Street of Boston, Whitfield submitted his requirements, the orders divided into thirds with one third sub-divided into halves. Items are listed on four ledger sheets two of which add up to about two thirds the total while two others represent one sixth each. These goods were destined for the Southern Cheyenne at Bent's Fort, (one third), the Arapaho and Northern Cheyenne at Fort St. Vrain (one sixth each), and for the Sioux at Fort Laramie (one third). Each list begins with dozens of butcher knives and ends with dozens of cow bells. Other items include square nails, gun flints, hand saw files, brass kettles, looking glasses, fly pans, needles, agate buttons, and finger rings. Shipping materials, casks, cases and hooping, are charged on the last line. Orders for Bent's Fort, Fort St. Vrain "A" and Fort St. Vrain "B" plus shipping to Fort Laramie comprise the transportation list. Apparently, annuity goods for the Northern Cheyenne and the Arapaho were marked separately though both were sent to St. Vrain's.

By May 1, Whitfield was in New York in the establishment of Grant & Barton, "Importers and jobbers of staple dry goods." Here he purchased blankets, beads, vermillion, thread, clothing, and many varieties and colors of cloth for "the Fort Laramie [Treaty] Indians." The total at Grant and Barton surpassed $10,000.while that at Callender, Rogers and Hilton amounted to around $2500. Whitfield seemed determined to oversee the process of procuring and shipping annuity goods personally. As with most government programs, accusations of graft and corruption flew at about the same rate as the opportunities for wrongdoing.

Of the latter, there were myriad. Jealousy among retailers provides an example. While Robert Campbell was regarded in Washington as a man of exceptional integrity, other St. Louis businessmen resented the monopoly Campbell exercised over this lucrative contract. Pierre Chouteau appears in the field correspondence to the Indian Commissioner for one year as a supplier of annuity goods. Not long after, a correspondent in Washington writes a mild reproof, stating that Mr. Campbell ought to be the supplier. It is not difficult to read between the lines of such correspondence and hear cries of "Foul! Foul!" from businessmen and traders whose interests were not served or whose livelihood was threatened by the annuity arrangements.

A between-the-lines reading of the letter Whitfield sent to his supervisor in the Office of Indian Affairs suggests his anxiety. It is dated May 1, 1854, New York.

Sir,

I returned here from Boston Saturday evening—I found Mssr. Calender, Rogers and Hilton ready to fill my bill. I purchased to the amount of funds set aside for hardware less about $400 which was to purchase brass wire. I declined taking the wire believing I could invest the amount in something of more value to the Indians on my arrival. I drafted a note to Mr. Wilson [axe manufacturer] directing him to forward the Axes here; enclosed I send you his answer—I shall not be able to remain here untill Mr. Wilson manufactures them and have so advised him. I am anxious to have the axes. Please direct me what to do. I suppose I can purchase them at some other place—; the Gunshells I shall... purchase if I can get the Guns that were left at Fort Atkinson now at Fort Riley. I will carry them to Fort Laramie. Mssr Grant & Barton are now packing some of my goods—and if the steamer arrives today which is now said to be in sight I will be able to ship every article from here this week. You may be assured I am as anxious to get off as any man could be. I have three or four days work to do at Westport before I leave—I will be in Washington I hope on Saturday. I think we shall have several days spare time before our goods can reach St. Louis, and I prefer to come by and *bring all my invoices—We have not decided what route to send the goods—we have several propositions and shall select the cheapest and most expeditious route having regard to responsibility.*

Respectfully yours,

J.W. Whitfield[2]

The illustration below, from the National Archives' records of the Upper Platte and Arkansas Agency show that annuities for the Cheyenne and Arapaho went to Fort St. Vrain:

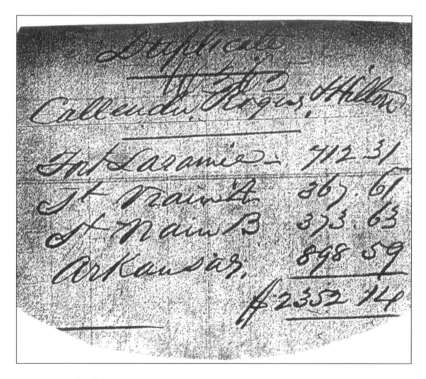

"Records of the Upper Platte and Arkansas Agency recall annuity goods for the Indians who signed the Fort Laramie Treaty, Sioux, Cheyenne and Arapaho; these were shipped to three locations with those going to Fort St. Vrain divided between the Arapaho and Northern Cheyenne. Courtesy Rocky Mountain National Archives, Denver, Colorado."

Whitfield had been officially confirmed to his appointment as Fitzpatrick's successor on May 20, 1854. On June 9th, 1854, wagons bound for Fort St. Vrain left Westport, Missouri. Whether these were the annuity goods from Boston and New York is not certain. Robert Campbell was paid $6847.57 by the U.S. government for goods to the Indians of the Upper Platte, referring to the Fort Laramie treaty. Totals to Campbell and the East coast merchants would be slightly more than $18,000 as stipulated by the treaty. It therefore seems probable that Campbell was shipping additional goods to meet the obligations to the Indians.

Like Fitzpatrick, Whitfield found the territory overwhelming. And, like many a contemporary administrator, he found his energies sapped by the seeming necessity to "put out fires." The "Grattan Massacre" near Fort Laramie provided a notorious case in point. A cow had strayed from, or perhaps just been left to die by, an emigrant group of Mormons. A Minneconjou Sioux living with the Dakotas near Fort Laramie, allegedly found, killed, and feasted upon the cow. The Mormons complained to the Laramie military and the Indians, realizing the breach of treaty this appeared to be, offered to make restitution. But Lieutenant Grattan, considered a hothead, with companions not altogether sober, called upon the Sioux in their encampment. Threats, outbursts of temper, and killings ensued, the Indians getting the best of it against the drunken interpreter and the disorganized soldiers. Whitfield was away at the moment of this incident. The Indians and the traders awaited his return with great anxiety, because he most probably would have been able to prevent the military solution which Lieutenant Grattan so ardently desired. Whitfield was at Fort St. Vrain at the time of the Grattan massacre, attending to business with the Cheyenne and Arapaho. When we consider that the Grattan massacre is often considered the inciting incident of a decade of warfare and hostility between the Sioux, their allies, such as the Cheyenne, and depredations committed by all sides, we can only admit that the government's refusal to hire assistant administrators for the outposts of the Upper

Platte and Arkansas Agency carried an incredibly high price in loss of life, health and happiness for those who might otherwise have lived in relative harmony.[3]

Whitfield reported to his supervisor in Washington, D.C. by way of a letter posted from Westport, MO, October 2nd, 1854, a "special report" in order to set the facts of the Grattan matter before his supervisors:

> On my way from Fort St. Vrain to Laramie I met about twenty-five lodges of Sioux Indians who informed me that a few days previous a Mormon train had stopped their . . . and that a lone cow strayed into the village and that a Minneconjue Sioux from the Upper Agency had killed and eat him. Two days afterwards Brev't Lt. Grattan with twenty-nine soldiers and his interpreter came down to demand the Indian who committed the depredation by killing the Mormon cow. The Indians refused to surrender and a fight ensued in which the Lt's interpreter and every man was killed. On my arrival at Fort Laramie I immediately commenced investigating the affair to ascertain all the facts connected with the fight. I sent for a number of the traders and others who were likely to know anything about it.

The Office of Indian Affairs was supplied with a paper storm of testimony and affidavits from traders around Fort Laramie. James Bordeaux acted as spokesman for the traders. The involvement of this group in what at first appears a dispute among Mormons, Indians, and the military at Fort Laramie suggests that government-supplied annuities to the Indians had cut into the traders' livelihood. Their complaints to Agent Whitfield perhaps aroused his suspicions that the traders, including the sutler at Fort Laramie, Seth Ward, had promoted the incident with the cow and the drunken soldiers in order to stir up trouble. The hypothesis is strengthened by the observation of Arapaho Indian historian, Margaret Coel, that the Indians formed their own trading networks during their latter years on the plains. Of course, the Indians had always traded, especially with the Mexicans, but also with allied tribes, for centuries before white traders came into the Rocky Mountain region. William Bent, through his Southern Cheyenne family, learned how to run his business from his in-laws. He did not merely impose white marketing techniques on the Mexicans and Indians who had arrived before the Bent, St. Vrain Co. However, the goods that Indians received from the government must have drastically reduced the demand by the Indians for goods which they once could obtain only from the independent traders at posts such as Fort Laramie, Fort St. Vrain, and Bent's Fort.

The following year, the Upper Platte and Arkansas Agency was officially divided, a change long overdue. A new man, Thomas Twiss, was installed at the Upper Platte, with headquarters at Fort Laramie. Twiss was the most colorful and intellectual of the three agents who served the Upper Platte Agency during the 1850's. He had graduated from West Point, second in his class, then resigned his commission. He taught natural sciences at South Carolina College. In 1850 he became resident and consulting engineer for the Buffalo and New York railroad, a position he left for his appointment as U.S.I.A., Upper Platte. He was well educated in the humanities—philosophy, history and literature—and was a skilled chess player.

He was, however, temperamentally unsuited for politics, being opinionated, stiff-necked, direct and authoritarian when his sympathies were involved, and reluctant to compromise. He seems to have played favorites with his friends among the traders at Fort Laramie and withheld favor from others. Shortly after his arrival at the Upper Platte, Twiss reported that Fort Laramie's sutler Seth Ward was a major troublemaker and he suspended his license to trade. Some of Twiss' rationale most probably lay in his inherited mess over the Grattan massacre. But, retribution came quickly and viciously. Twiss was accused of malfeasance. Ward and his friends testified that they had seen a bale of buffalo robes in Twiss' quarters. Was Twiss trading on the side and "selling"

Indian goods back to the Indians for personal profit? General Harney, who had led a punitive expedition against the Sioux in the winter of 1855, disliked Twiss because of his partisanship to the Indians' welfare and lack of cooperation with the War Department. He fired Twiss from his position. Twiss went to Washington D.C. where he managed to convince Indian Commissioner Manypenny of his innocence, have his name cleared, and be reappointed.[4]

On March 7th 1856, Twiss wrote a letter to the Commandant at Fort Laramie, Colonel Hoffman, whom he disliked. From "Bissonnette's camp near the Fort," Twiss announced that he had instructions from Commissioner Manypenny concerning the establishment of the Cheyenne and Araphao Indian Agency at Fort St. Vrain as of the previous October. It was Twiss' intention "to repair to that Agency with . . . the Indian Goods and public property in my charge. . . . The Agency of the Sioux Bands of the North Platte is hereby closed until further orders and instruction are received from the President" (see photostat frontspiece to this chapter).

The letter is a symptom of Twiss' predicament within the Upper Platte Agency.

When it became known that General Harney had led a force to punish the Sioux for "depredations," Twiss insisted that his Indians were peaceful. He urged them to remain south of the Platte, which the majority agreed to do. Burton S. Hill, writing of the Harney foray against the Sioux in *The Great Plains Journal* explains:

> Yet on September 2, 1855, in spite of his mandate, a large portion of the Brule band, under Little Thunder, was encamped on Blue Water Creek about six miles northwest of Ash Hollow. A full account of General Harney's attack, which followed, may be read in Hafen and Young's *Fort Laramie*. In a writing entitled *Our Indian Wards,* (Cincinnati, 1880), 159 which is mentioned in Hoopes, Commissioner Manypenny considered Harney's attack "cruelly unjust," but, as pointed out by Hoopes, Little Thunder was on the

north side of the Platte. Even the Indians recognized this, and in their report to Agent Twiss maintained that General Harney was in the right. This the Agent reported to the Commissioner of Indian Affairs on October 1, 1855 (Hill 87).

Apparently, Commissioner Manypenny's order concerning Fort St. Vrain was meant to keep the Indians south of the Platte, *per* Twiss' recommendation. The letter in which Twiss declares the Sioux agency closed and the Arapaho and Cheyenne agency established at Fort St. Vrain had a complex set of reasons behind it. One was, of course, to sidestep the aggressive policies of the War Department and its generals by drawing the Sioux south of the Platte. Another was to remove the pressures of the squabbling traders around Fort Laramie from Twiss' long list of problems. Twiss had worked tirelessly to establish peace and equilibrium during those months between the late fall of 1855 (Harney's Battle at Ash Hollow had occurred hardly more than a month after Twiss' arrival as the new Indian agent) and over the spring and summer of 1856. His situation was extremely fragile; it would not have taken much interference from traders like Seth Ward or James Bordeaux to confound the entire process. No wonder Twiss considered Ward a troublemaker or sought allies among traders like Bissonnette who seems to have had a more realistic grasp of just how explosive the circumstances at Fort Laramie were. Hill goes on to explain:

> After Ash Hollow, General Harney and Agent Twiss disagreed bitterly as to the proper means of restoring peace. So bitter was the dispute, that Twiss prevented representatives of the Brule and Oglala nations from attending the Harney negotiations conducted at Fort Pierre on March 1, 1856. Even though the Fort Pierre Treaty was fairly well maintained for several years, it was never agreed to by Agent Twiss, nor ratified by the Senate. And, Twiss did not make himself any more popular with General Harney, nor

with Colonel William Hoffman, in command of Fort Laramie, by this recommendation that the trader's licence of Ward and Guerrier be revoked. Twiss had become convinced that these traders were trading with the Indians in violation of the [alcohol prohibition] law (Hill 88).

Sometime before March of 1856, Twiss had married an Oglala woman, a daughter of Standing Elk, who had, it was rumored, benefitted greatly from his son-in-laws's access to the U.S. government supplies and annuities. The South Platte trader, John Simpson Smith, interpreter for the Northern Cheyenne, testified on March 3, 1856, that the "Cheyenne were complaining because they were not receiving their proportionate share of the goods from Agent Twiss" (90). Twiss' letter on repairing to Fort St. Vrain is dated just four days later. The implication, for anyone wishing to synthesize these documents from groups who possessed inflamatory and competing agendas and interests, is that Twiss had donated some Cheyenne annuity goods to his in-laws. Furthermore, John Simpson Smith, who knew Seth Ward and Guerrier even better than he knew Twiss, was a trader himself. He might be thought to have had a heavy ax to grind. And since Smith's headquarters was usually at Fort St. Vrain, Twiss may have written his letter of March 7, 1856 in response to this kind of accusation, to put to rest any complaints the Cheyenne might have by removing the goods from near Fort Laramie to Fort St. Vrain. The Cheyenne could see for themselves, then, the fairness of the distributions of goods.

Before Twiss could follow through with his intentions to move the agency to Fort St. Vrain, he had to clarify whether a general in the War Department had the authority to hire and fire Indian agents. And, as Twiss' Washington inquiry ended, Harney did not. And, in the eventuality, he did not remove goods and property to Fort St. Vrain. The old adobe fort had been a convenient way to triangulate Twiss' dilemma.

Upon his return to his agency in late June, 1856, the troubles had multiplied, with reports of Indians' harrassing

of emigrant trains, robberies, kidnappings, and murders—
Indian depredations and atrocities. In September 1856, at
the Upper Platte Agency, Twiss met with Indian leaders and
"as a result of these councils a general cessation of hostilities
was brought about" (88). For the next year the Cheyene
remained peaceful, until they were attacked at Solomon's
Fork in the summer of 1857 by the cavalry troops led by
Colonel Edwin Vose Sumner and Major Sedgwick, an ill-
advised and "farcical" campaign which caused reprisals and
lasting bitterness.

The new administration under President James
Buchanan gave Twiss his opportunity to yield his office to a
new appointee. By this time, Twiss had taken his agency to
Deer Creek, a hundred miles northwest of Fort Laramie.
There he stayed with his family for some time, and then
moved to the Rulo, Nebraska area in later years. He became
an eccentric. Occasionally he would visit Fort Laramie, a
buckskin and mocassin-clad figure with curly white hair
down his back. He could speak eloquently about Grant's
strategies in the Civil War, explaining to his listeners the
comparisons of these with those of Napoleon seventy-five
years before. He had, like some of those perplexing young
rebels of the American 1960's, gone to the Third World like
Peace Corps Voluneers and stayed as an exile from his
birthright and cultural roots upon a decision to "go native."
And, like an American reincarnation of an ancient Socrates,
he clung to his love of philosophizing, dying with honor
according to those who knew him best—but leaving a wife
and children in deepest destitution.

Thus, Fort St. Vrain never became an Indian agency with
a resident agent. It was a useful site in the 1850's for distrib-
uting annuity goods to the area Indians—and as a headquarters for transient traders and peddlars—as well as for the
"Rawhide" hands who now drove the Texas cattle northward
to the rail centers at Omaha or even Chicago. For them, it was
a hotel without a proprietor, but with abundant grass along
the watercourses, it was for the cattlemen very good camp. In
1857 Edwin Vose Sumner used it as a base of operations

during his and Sedgwick's campaign against the Cheyenne. No recorded Indian battles occurred at the site, however. In the following year, the entire neighborhood around the old South Platte forts would be transformed as the Gold Regions of the Rockies commenced to draw hundred of thousands of immigrants seeking riches along the South Platte, called the Fourth Eldorado in the advertisements in the East, and up and down the affluents—Clear Creek, Cherry Creek, St. Vrain Creek, Cache la Poudre—where glimmering nuggets the size of a man's fist were thought to be laying around waiting for gold-seekers—like Easter eggs in a hunt by toddlers.

Notes to Chapter Five
Indian Agency on the South Platte

[1]Fitzpatrick's biography, *Broken Hand: The Life of Thomas Fitzpatrick, Mountain Man, Giude and Indian Agent.* Lincoln: Nebraska UP, 1981, 325–336.

[2]Upper Platte and Arkansas Agency, Correspondence from the Field. Denver, Co: National Archives, Rocky Mountain Region. Mf 889. All records quoted and referenced to the Upper Platte and Arkansas in this chapter are contained on this microfilm.

[3]Accounts of the Grattan Massacre have been published in many sources. This summary is drawn from Lloyd E. McCann, *The Grattan Massacre,* reprinted from *Nebraska History,* 37:1 (March, 1956).

[4]Information about Thomas Twiss, U.S.I.A. has been synthesized from several sources, including LeRoy Hafen, *Mountain Men and the Fur Trade,* volume III, 369 ff; from *The Great Plains Journal,* by Burton Hill, "Thomas I. Twiss, Indian Agent," 6:2 (Spring 1967) 85–96. See also Thrapp, *Frontier Biography,* "Twiss," III, 1453–1454.

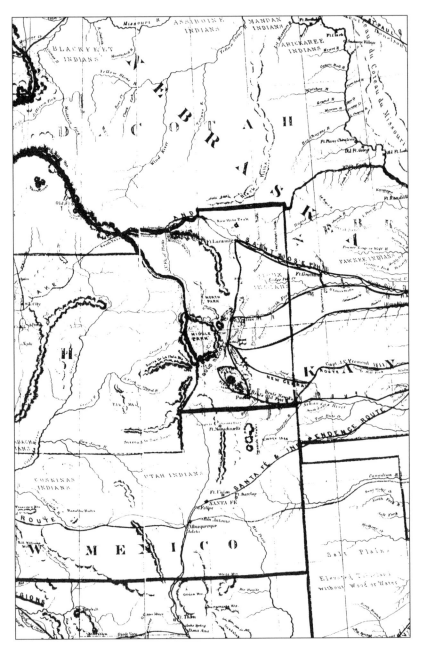

Map showing proposed Jefferson Territory, drawn by D. McGowan, 1859, based on then current territorial maps of the western U.S.

108

𝒪9. 𝒯he St. 𝒱rain Claim Club

In the late 1850's Fort St. Vrain became a significant governmental center. The ad hoc process by which it achieved such a focus for white settlement is a case-in-point and model of much western settlement.

A dozen years after the Bent, St. Vrain trading post had been closed, and two years before Colorado became a territory, the St. Vrain valleys attracted immigrants who at last intended to settle and to stay. Furthermore, since, according to the treaty of Fort Laramie, 1851, the Arapaho and Cheyenne Indians retained the land along the eastern base of the Rockies between the Platte and Arkansas rivers, certain problems attended upon processes of settlement.

One local historian, Cleon Roberts[1] in his bicentennial history of Fort Lupton, observed that, as the American west attracted white settlement, actions always *preceded* legal sanctions. The word "preemption" sums up the concept at the heart of this. White settlers exercised what they themselves called "squatter's rights." For the South Platte valleys of northeastern Colorado, this generally meant that the site a family—or more likely a man whose family awaited his decision "back east"—selected for a homestead appeared to be no-man's-land, might be Indian land but later on might not: so, a person's claim would establish buyer's rights in the future. The claimant "preempted" Indians, railroad men, miners, other farmers and all other comers.

Claims to 160 acres had, it seems, legal precedent in the 1841 Preemption Act under which some U.S. public land to the east had been settled. Of course, this law had no bearing in the South Platte valleys of 1859, but the specifying of 160 acres as a "claim" reveals that the 1841 legislation was being used as a model. Unlike the later Homestead Act (1862) which was a benefit for Union Civil War veterans, preemption claimants were supposed to pay $1.25 per acre as well as make demonstrated improvements. Whether the first settlers did have to pay is doubtful, for their membership in a claim club constituted their entitlement to the acreage. Thus, even though most immigrants during the 1850's knew the South Platte Valley was "Indian Territory," the "preempting" of a mere one hundred and sixty acres from land that had, somewhere in descriptions of the Louisiana Purchase, seemingly been declared "public" appeared insignificant, or if significant, surmountable. The settlers who held Manifest Destiny as a first principle could find the absence of law and order in the mining towns appalling, but could also find loopholes in existing territorial laws by which to justify their exercise of squatters' rights. The prairie was vast and the Indians, who had no semblance of a consistent foreign policy, used the land, after all, only as a private hunting club or (whites rationalized) for their petty intertribal wars.

The legal issues are exceedingly difficult. Many recent historians emphasize, however, the *illegal* nature of those first white settlers' claims in 1858, '59 and '60. The Indians did not relinquish that land until the treaty of Fort Wise in 1861. The newcomers, looking for ranching and farming possibilities, as well as gold mines, were "squatting" on Indian land, territory where jurisdictions—federal, territorial and tribal—were confused, ambiguous, even contradictory. In 1854, the Kansas and Nebraska Territories were established west of the Missouri and included most of present eastern Colorado. In addition, Kansas established Arapaho County as its westernmost region. In 1854 there were no permanent white settlements that could take advantage of this. By 1858, when Kansas became a state, the boundary was drawn on the eastern edge of Arapaho County, which then became truly a no-man's land. Furthermore, the new territorial governments were too preoccupied with matters (slavery and alcohol abuse were high on the list) near to and east of the Missouri River to govern the land at the western-most reaches. The great distances between the eastern Nebraska boundary near Omaha and the western one along the Rockies made the laws unenforceable even if enforcement had been a major concern. The Kansas Territorial codes explicitly stated that territorial law would not apply on treaty-designated Indian land. There was, for this reason, no administered "law," and almost no sanctioned territorial governance throughout the eastern half of present Colorado though it was nominally within Nebraska and Kansas territorial boundaries.

The map below shows the Kansas-Nebraska territorial boundaries along the 40th parallel. It is shown here through the courtesy of the U.S. Geologic Survey and the "Historic Trails Maps" project completed by Glenn R. Scott. When the first survey was completed, the 40th parallel ran through Boulder, Colorado and the street over it, aptly named Baseline

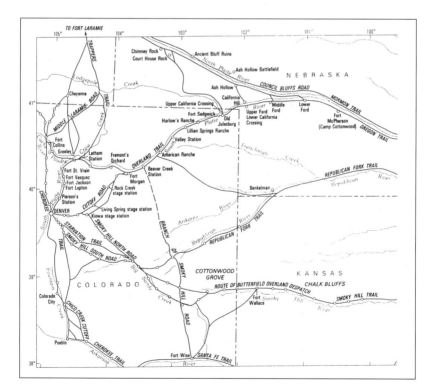

Road, comes to its western end at the foot of the mountain range, the Flatirons. In the gold rush era of 1858-59, this division between the Kansas and Nebraska territories added great confusion to an already perplexing questions of governance and land, public, Indian or privately owned.

The first farmers and ranchers, speculators and miners in the area of the South Platte and St. Vrain valleys did not make claims and exercise squatters' rights solely on their own initiative. They visited land offices in the east, read guide books and newspapers, often listening to the advice of former mountain men. A few them had seen the lush valley while on cattle drives from Texas to rail heads in Chicago or Omaha. These would return to investigate ranching possibilities; some would stay. In northeastern Colorado their primary local mentor was a man famous for his pioneering, journalistic and "booster" activities—Mr. William Byers, founder of the region's first newspaper, *The Rocky Mountain News*. He was a leader in "colonizing" activities for which he used Old Fort St. Vrain (among other places) as a center.

The most complete biography of William Byers appears in the centennial history of Byers and Co's newspaper by Robert Perkin: *The Rocky Mountain News: The First One Hundred Years*. Of Byers' "colonizing" activities, Perkin says:.

> Busy as he was with printing and publishing, Byers as usual was neck deep in other activities. . . . The colonization business was good. Once Byers had Greeley well established [1871] he journeyed to Chicago and sold 55 thousand acres to . . . men who moved west in 1871 and founded the town of Longmont. The dynamic Byers thus was involved directly or indirectly in the establishment of at least five Colorado towns: Denver, Greeley, Longmont, Meeker, and Hot Sulphur Springs. And it was he who gave Central City its name (Perkin 13).

Byers also gave Estes Park its name; Joel Estes was among Byers' friends—and Byers liked to hike in the area,

112

being among the first to climb nearly to the summit of Long's Peak. Byers was truly a mountaineer and not, like Fremont, one in name only. He served as secretary to the Platte River Land Company which founded Platteville in 1871. His activities in Denver and at Old Fort St. Vrain preceded by more than 10 years his colonization activities on behalf of Platteville, Greeley and Longmont.

One of Byers' outstanding personal characteristics was a restlessness that kept him "perambulating" on constant excursions however brief, often arduous, and sometimes exceedingly long. In his early twenties, for example, in 1851, he walked the Oregon Trail to the Far West. There, in Oregon Territory he worked as a surveyor's assistant, helping lay out the first towns in present Washington state. His remuneration for this was not coinage but a state of the art set of surveying equipment, a much-admired solar compass. Byers then journeyed down the coast to California, and visited Sacramento where he presumably learned something about organizing mining towns and miners' vigilante justice. He returned to his parents' Iowa farm by way of the Panama Isthmus and the eastern half of the United States. Soon he moved to an upstart Missouri river hamlet called Omaha where he opened a land office that served also as a focus for informal politics and planning. Byers established himself in a surveying business, platting out the new city, partnering with an attorney named Poppleton, who later became important in the railroad's real estate industry.

After 1854, his land company sold lots in Omaha and Byers built one of the town's first five homes. He helped establish the Papplo Claim Club; he ran for and won a seat in the first Nebraska Territorial legislature. He also encouraged and modeled investment in embryonic commerce and industry in Omaha. Such promotional activity had become a standard procedure, the protocol of frontier settlement, and it was the formula Byers applied to his new projects at Fort St. Vrain in the Pikes Peak region (eastern Colorado) when he arrived two years later, in April of 1859.[2]

His first overt sign of interest in eastern Colorado was his signature on a Pikes Peak regional "Guidebook," one of eighteen such pamphlets (by as at least as many authors) still in existence, according to LeRoy Hafen. With co-author Mr. Jonathan Kellom, Byers' "Guide to the Gold Regions of Kansas and Nebraska" encourages goldseekers to prospect in this "Eldorado of the South Platte." Byers explains what tools and supplies to carry, what milestones and camp-grounds exist along the routes. He himself favors the Oregon Trail to Fort Laramie, then south to Fort St. Vrain on the Trappers' or Cherokee Trail. But he also notes alternative possibilities. He quotes testimonials from a variety of news-papers published in Plattsmouth, Leavenworth and St. Louis, regarding the availability of gold. Summarizing an article from the *Nebraska News* of January 1, 1859, he notes, "Several person have arrived at Plattsmouth and Pacific City [Iowa] bringing with them numerous specimens—glorious, golden nuggets! Our fellow citizen, Judge Bennet, saw one of the specimens containing nineteen dollars, picked up from among others scattered around miscellaneously and loosely." Judge Hiram Bennet also moved to the Pikes Peak region in the fall of '59 and of him more will be reported subsequently.

On January 26, 1859, Byers wrote his co-author Kellom that "a party came in yesterday; they brought specimens of very rich gold quartz which are on exhibition here. . . ."[3] The guidebook reports that miners are making at least two dol-lars a day and that the best finds have been up the Cache la Poudre river (the most northeasterly of the gold-bearing streams flowing into the South Platte river 55 miles north of Cherry Creek). Thus, the 1859 rush to the Rockies of approx-imately 100,000 prospectors sounds familiar—in the manner of modern "media" events. For, the fact of gold in the Rocky Mountains had been reported for more than half a century before the 1859 "stampede." As early as 1803, Zebulon Pike's exploratory group had reported signs. William Gilpin, geolo-gist and geographer, wrote enthusiastically about the gold in the Rockies. However, it required bank failures, a financial depression along the Missouri settlements—and the threat of a Civil War to give a "push" to those who wished to capital-ize on the "pull" of Rocky Mountain riches.

Like Charles Fremont, Byers founded a successful career upon a marriage into a politically astute family. In November, 1854, he acquired a bride, Elizabeth Sumner, whose grandfather, Robert Lucas, had been governor of Ohio and the first territorial governor of Iowa. The kind of savvy it takes to set up the machinery of governance, towns and Euro-American settlement ran deeply in her family traditions. In addition to what Byers learned about surveying and organizing settlements in the Oregon Territory, he could now borrow from his new, young, ambitious associates and his highly respected in-laws. Byers and his associates, Bella Hughes, Hiram J. Graham, D.C. Oakes, Hiram Bennet and a few others, created on-paper towns and counties. They took the remarkable step of creating an entire territory, in order to secure western lands for the United States, and, perhaps, a real estate empire for themselves. Fort St. Vrain was selected as the site to bring order to western Nebraska Territory, or perhaps it would be more accurate to say that it was self-selected as a site because, in the midst of mostly nothingness, Fort St. Vrain was *there.*

The area around Fort St. Vrain, one imagines, in the winter of '58 must have been a "tent city." St. Vrain Creek, flowing into the South Platte just south of the fort, was a favorite waterway for the panners of gold. Many of these, disappointed by the sparse offerings of the creek itself, gave up in disgust, cursed Byers, Oakes and all writers of "Guidebooks" to riches. They joined the 70,000 "go-backs" so roundly reviled by the *Rocky Mountain News.* Some of the remainder hiked up the St. Vrain to the point where it joins Boulder Creek and continued to the foothills from there. The most successful of the seekers who used this route was Captain Aiken and his party, who found a vein worth developing on a hill they named Gold Hill, not far from the town called Golden City. Thus, Fort St. Vrain, like Denver City, was part of a rim on a geographic "wheel" the spokes of which were gold-bearing streams rushing east toward the South Platte and the eastern Colorado prairies.

All this brings us to the greatest truism in Colorado history: the gold rush of 1858-59 was the beginning of Colorado settlement.

The activities of white settlers along the South Platte in northern Kansas Territory (Denver) and southern Nebraska Territory (Fort St. Vrain) in the late 1850's opened doors for the thriving colony-towns—Greeley, Evans, Longmont—of northeastern Colorado (southwest of the Oregon Trail) and set the stage for the actual county, territorial and state governments of the 1860's and 70's. In this way, the earliest white settlements of Colorado, the fur trade posts of Bent's Fort and Fort St. Vrain, were linked to the later civic centers developed in the river valleys and plains of northeastern Colorado.

The lynch pin upon which the settlements could be created and flourish in the neighborhoods of the old adobe trading post was the Jefferson Territory. Since this was a paper-only governmental unit, short-lived and apparently a failure, some modern historians prefer to give it a paragraph, apologize for the false start, the anomaly at the foundation of the state of Colorado—and move quickly on to the success stories of Denver and the achievement of Colorado statehood in 1876. Others recognize that it was the link between being and non-being for the Colorado Territory of 1861. They understand that the Jefferson Territory was a necessary—if thin— piece of paper, without which the fate of the Indians and Euro-American settlers might have been quite different.

Old Fort St. Vrain was included in the plans for the government tentatively called "State of Jefferson." The first edition of the *Rocky Mountain News,* issued April 23, 1859 "contains proceedings of the convention that proposed and outlined a state to be called Jefferson." On this date, Byers was already en route to the central Rockies. The fact that the story had been previously typeset in Omaha, ready to be printed in the Pikes Peak region, however, meant that this "news" item began as a convenient prophecy, or, we must understand, a manifestation of the political aims for the sake of which Byers' "was instructed" to purchase the printing press from one Peter Sarpy of Bellevue and install a newspaper in the Pikes Peak region at a location yet to be decided. Robert Perkin states that several sites in the region were still under consideration:

"[Byers'] several reminiscences of the founding [of the newspaper] show clearly that he did not know precisely where he was going and that he planned to pick whatever location seemed most auspicious. Under other circumstances the *Rocky Mountain News* might have been published in Golden City or Boulder City, both struggling into existence at this time, or at the old fur trade post of Fort St. Vrain or at Arapahoe, a ghost town several miles west of Denver . . ." (36).

The first edition of the *News* also stated its mission in terms of service to the gold seekers. In this endeavor, his newspaper encouraged agricultural activity to provide food for miners, settlers and communities such as Denver City. It emphasized the primacy of the mining industry, the needs of the prospectors for legal protection, assuming the right of the miners to pursue get-rich-quick dreams as part of the legacy of the continent. And, in the months and years that followed, the *News* routinely printed stories of large-scale slaughter of whites by Indians, as evidence of treaty violations that would justify white settlement under forfeiture of Indian land. The *Rocky Mountain News* covered every rumor of "depredations" by the "savages" while treating with silence any voices which pointed out the illegality of establishing a territorial government on Indian land.

There was, some government leaders believed, simply too much at stake to dally over questions of Indian rights. To the east, Kansas and Nebraska Territorial legislators were even then debating whether the new western territories would be brought into the union as slave states or free. The unity of the nation lay at the heart of issues concerning the disposition of the lands of the West, of unorganized portions of the Louisiana purchase. They also believed that if the gold fields of the Kansas and Nebraska Territories were not brought under the governance of the United States, southern interests would soon exploit them and perhaps pay for a successful war of secession with these riches. Thus, the mission statement in the first edition of the *News,* typeset far in advance of its printing in Denver, frankly stated the intentions to oversee

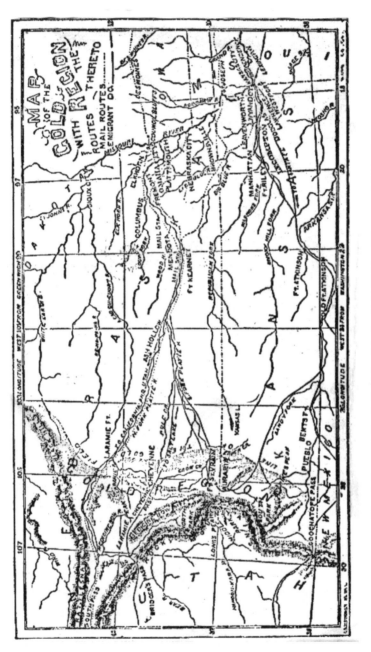

Map in Byers-Kellom's Guidebook to the Gold Fields of Kansas and Nebraska.

and promote the success of individual gold seekers without commenting upon these forestalling or preempting tactics against the Confederacy.

On April 15th, Byers' two-wagon party reached Fort St. Vrain. He had left his wife in Omaha and come west with her four Sumner brothers, plus a newspaperman named Thomas Gibson. They had planned to do a little prospecting along the Cache la Poudre, an affluent of the South Platte, using Fort St. Vrain as a headquarters. However, Byers got word at Fort St. Vrain that one Mr. John Merrick was about to launch the region's first newspaper. The aging Bent, St. Vrain mail carrier, "Uncle Dick" Wootton offered Byers the upper loft of his outfitting store, the "first two-story building in Denver," as a press room. Uncle Dick was prepared to stir up a little excitement in Denver City and Auraria by sponsoring, and no doubt making book for, a contest to see which of the two papers would hit the streets *first*. Such circumstances led Byers to bring the press to Auraria-Denver City.

Byers had no journalism experience. He was a real estate agent and surveyor by training and trade and he quickly turned the day-to-day operations of the newspaper over to Gibson and composed editorials advancing his party agenda—important associations with Republicans, Masons, in-laws, friends and business associates' "manifest destiny." Meanwhile he "perambulated," making haste to organize "conventions" to legitimize the envisioned state of Jefferson. It had come into being less than a month after his arrival, on June 6, 1859—and he helped to elect representatives to Congress from the embryonic state.

The shadows of the Missouri Compromise draped gloomily over all pioneer hopes to establish new territories, especially after 1854 when the Kansas and Nebraska Territories extended, on paper anyhow, to the eastern base of the Rockies. For, Congressmen in Washington were reluctant to add voting power to the "other" side—north, south, free, slave. So, chances of getting a distinct Territory of Colorado (though it had no name in those days, and might have been Colona, El Dorado or a number of other possibilities—even "Bill Williams" was suggested), chances of getting Congressional

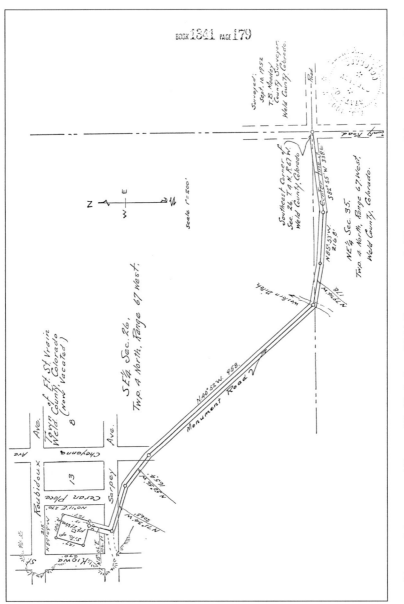

Picture of the proposed Town of St. Vrain from Weld County records. The streets are named for mountain men whom Byers admired as well as local Indian groups near Omaha and Fort St. Vrain.

approval for a Jefferson Territory or any Territory were nil. The eastern Nebraska-western Iowa entrepreneurs who came in '58 and '59—Byers, Oakes, Graham, Bennet, Hughes, Cook and others—understood the wise tactics of organizing first and seeking governmental blessing second.

So, Byers had himself elected Territorial Surveyor and in the three weeks following his arrival at Cherry Creek, he had mapped out the boundaries, showing the Jefferson Territory (it had been voted to start modestly at this level rather than as a "state") to include parts of eastern Utah, southern Wyoming, all of Colorado and parts of western Kansas and Nebraska.

Four months after that, October 6, 1859, Byers was back at Fort St. Vrain to form the St. Vrain Claim Club and to create an "on-paper" county of St. Vrain and a township and county seat for that portion of the Jefferson Territory north of the 40th parallel, nominally in western Nebraska Territory.

Minutes were kept of this first meeting of the St. Vrain Claim Club and of subsequent actions taken. The resulting document, the *St. Vrain Record Book,* was first stored in the Weld County courthouse, and then placed in an abandoned missile silo west of Greeley. Copies are available in the archives of the Colorado State Historical Society's Stephen Hart library, as well as at the Greeley Municipal Museum. This *Record Book* tells us something about the colonization effort near Fort St. Vrain in the fifteen months before Colorado became a Territory. The first meeting, described briefly, explains:

> At a meeting of the Citizens of Saint Vrain held Oct. 6th, 1859, C.P. Hall was duly chosen Chairman and H.J. Graham, Secretary. The object of the meeting having been by the Chairman stated, to be for the purpose of organizing a claim club, laying off Saint Vrain County, and Electing a Recorder for the same. After which Mr. Byers moved that each claimant be entitled to 160 acres on the public lands; the same to be staked and plainly marked, and recorded, which shall be sufficient to hold it valid until June 1st, 1860, when further improvements must be made.

Above motion adopted. Mr. Byers moved also that the jurisdiction of this club shall be co-extensive with the County of Saint Vrain (in Nebraska Territory) to embrace not less than twenty four miles square with the town of Saint Vrain near the centre.

Motion adopted unanimously. Moved by P.G. Lowe that H.J. Graham be elected Recorder for St. Vrain County, and that he be allowed one dollar for each paper recorded; motion adopted and H.J. Graham declared duly elected Recorder. After which meeting adjourned, Sine Die (*St. Vrain Record Book* 1).

Notices in the *Record Book's* following ten pages describe claims and claimants, numbering 1–26, dating from September 30, 1859 (a week before the Claim Club's first recorded meeting) until February 21, 1860. Several other claims, quit claims and land transfers are recorded, as are sundry business matters requiring attention by these first "acting county commissioners" of the county that—in a way—never was.

The language of parliamentary procedure, election of officers and even condition of land entitlement is carefully chosen to lend legitimacy to this process which had no genuine legal basis and no recourse to official land surveys—still non-existent. One is reminded of a parallel instance in the mid 1980's when one U.S. Senator grumbled about relinquishing the Panama Canal back to the Panamanians on the grounds that "we stole it fair and square." Since there was no official survey of this land which belonged by treaty to the Arapaho and Cheyenne Indians, the St. Vrain Claim Club had to rely on crude descriptions of feet and rods from natural landmarks, rivers, streams, boulders—and the adobe walls of Old Fort St. Vrain. Hence a typical claim read:

Albert Thorn claims one hundred and sixty Acres of the public lands in Saint Vrain County N.T., Lying south of the Town of Saint Vrain and described as follows to wit, Commencing at the South West corner of the town of Saint Vrain, thence East on the South line of said town (as pr plat) one mile, thence South one fourth of a mile, thence West of the Platt River, thence North down along the said platt River to the place of Beginning. This claim taken, staked and marked, August 28th, 1860 (19).

Some claims were staked thus on islands in the South Platte river which have since disappeared into its sandy bottoms. The *St. Vrain Record Book* is the oldest surviving document of its kind in Colorado. The St. Vrain Claim Club was perhaps the first of several claim clubs founded. Only the Arapahoe County Claim Club may have been earlier, but its record book has disappeared, apparently stolen from the Denver Public Library's Western History Department. Thus, the precise date of its founding is not known, although its by-laws have been preserved in an article about it in *Colorado Magazine.*

At the same time that Byers, Hiram J. Graham and others were creating the St. Vrain Claim Club, another of Colorado's prominent pioneers had arrived at Fort St. Vrain: Hiram Pitt Bennet, an attorney from Nebraska City and Plattsmouth who had served as Speaker of the House in the first Nebraska Territorial legislature of which Byers was also a member. Bennet's autobiography, published by the Colorado Historical Society in 1988, recounts his journey across the Platte River Road (North and South Platte rivers) in the fall of '59: "After thirty-five days of weary travel, we reached the abandoned old fort of St. Vrain, near [present] Platteville, in the early part of October. . . .We remained in camp at the fort for a two weeks' rest" (Lyendecker 69). It appears that Bennet was at Fort St. Vrain at the same time the Claim Club was founded. Being the only genuine lawyer in the vicinity, Bennet probably at least witnessed the proceedings. He does not mention the events surrounding the establishment of the Jefferson Territory, but in his memoir he states: "I had started [in Denver] a movement for a regular People's Court . . . The court followed the Iowa statutes since they were the only ones in town. They were taken from my law library. Being by far the largest and most valuable collection—fourteen volumes—they caused me to be regarded as the legal oracle of the country" (Lyendecker 74).

Bennet had, in the years that followed, often witnessed the same paperwork that Byers and his associates signed, but Bennet adds, "I was never part of Byers' inner circle." Bennet was, however, a cousin of D.C. Oakes and a friend of Hiram J. Graham. Byers, Bennet, and all community leaders in Arapaho and St. Vrain counties shared similar ambitions to bring white governance to the region and the legal structures which that entailed. In the courts, Bennet fought the outlaws just as Byers and Gibson fought them with the press. Bennet was staunchly an admirer of Abe Lincoln, a promoter of the Union cause, and was not above serving three or four kegs of whiskey to soften up Denverites to the flying of "Old Glory" in order to sort out who was on the right side of the issue. Bennet remained tactfully silent on the issue of Indian claims, but clearly someone had to install law and order. Bennet wrote:

> At the time [formation of the Jefferson Territory, June-October, 1859] . . . all the country that is now known as Colorado was without legally established law, whether federal, state or territorial. It is true that nominally Denver was then in what was known as the county of Arapahoe of the territory of Kansas. But when, a short time before, Kansas had been admitted as a state, its western boundary had been established along the east line of Arapahoe County. Between this time and the organization of the territory of Colorado in 1861, the large population from the eastern states who had rushed into the country during the Pikes Peak gold excitement found themselves living in a "no man's land." Deprived of all law and authority from without, the people fell back on the right of self-defense and established their own laws and tribunals (Lyendecker 73–74).

This succinct description tells us the justification for Claim Clubs and People's and Miner's Courts. Eventually some Claim Clubs were taken over by individuals as rough and careless of law as any hardened criminal. Vigilante justice got a bad name because of this and Byers and Bennet were criticized for "supporting" such rabble. Their intentions, however, were to promote peaceful settlement, and as so often happens with idealists and visionaries, events get far out of their control.

The U.S. government, meanwhile, would not recognize the Jefferson Territory, and Congress refused to seat its elected representatives. However, Byers and Gibson relabeled the *Rocky Mountain News* (which was at first imprinted with K.T. for "Kansas Territory") with "Denver, J.T." until, in 1861, it was appropriate to change it to C.T. for the Colorado Territory. The latter was officially recognized and its delegates to Congress, including Judge Hiram Bennet, were seated in Washington. Thus ended the Jefferson Territory, which was "not-very-effective" by the judgment of some historians. Most agree, though, that it "had more or less bridged the gap between the indifference of Kansas and the creation by Congress of the Colorado Territory."[4]

Fort St. Vrain's status was not quite such a muddle. Byers and his circle do not seem to have insisted on creating an issue about its connections to larger governmental bodies, although it was related to the proposed Jefferson Territory. Local policing seems to have been the primary goal, and it was sufficient to the purpose of creating local law and order to set up a county government there.

The charter members of the St. Vrain Claim Club seem to have been recruited by Byers and Co. from among residents of the Auraria-Cherry Creek vicinity. Hiram J. Graham, P.G. Lowe and Byers himself staked claims but, rather in the manner of absentee landlords, might not have occupied their claims personally. A possible exception is Graham, whose name appears in the *St. Vrain Record Book* on various documents which he witnessed as county clerk, but he may also have operated a drug store in Denver City. In any case, he eventually returned to the Omaha area. Permanent residency notwithstanding, several of the charter signers-on were famous—or became so—in the lore of Western Americana. For example, Pike Vasquez: His uncle was Louis Vasquez, founder of the fur trade post seven miles south of Old Fort St. Vrain, the first of the four South Platte trading posts. Today, it is the only one of the four forts with the physical semblance of the originals. Fort Vasquez, reconstructed in 1935 as a Works Progress Administration project to ease the depression, is one of the Colorado Historical Society's regional properties, the only one north of Denver. In 1964 a modern museum building was dedicated on site by CHS to educate visitors about the fur trade commerce, the adobe posts along the South Platte, and the lifestyle of the Plains Indian groups, especially Northern Cheyenne and Arapaho, who lived along the South Platte and its affluent creeks.

Fort Vasquez, a familiar sight to thousands of commuters daily, is situated adjacent to U.S. Highway 85 (the Canadian-American Highway) and the Union Pacific line from Denver to Cheyenne. Now, passers-by who wish to know what Fort St. Vrain looked like in its heyday will find at the rebuilt Fort Vasquez, the only remaining representative of the old South Platte adobe forts. Visitors to Fort St. Vrain's commemorative site and markers will experience, however, the *feel* of the 1840's neighborhood, a near-pristine place beneath the sublime peaks of the Never-Summer range and a hundred yards from the calm, winding South Platte river. Ironically, the same causes for Fort St. Vrain's true abandonment—i.e., transportation lines built four to five miles east of it—also constitute it value as an historical site worthy of a visitor's time, reminiscent of an era long gone.

Although Pike Vasquez is listed as a founding member of the St. Vrain Claim Club, he may not have been at the meeting. He managed a mercantile business, established in Denver City where his famous name enhanced his prospects. However, Fort Vasquez was still considered the family property which is the basis for Vasquez' membership, and that of his famous uncle Louis, if not their active participation, in the Claim Club.

Another St. Vrain Claim Club charter member who achieved lasting fame was P.G. Lowe. It was he who nominated H.J. Graham as the Claim Club's recorder. Lowe's journal about life in the pre-Civil War American West relates his experiences from 1849-1854 and is titled *Five Years A Dragoon: And Other Adventures on the Great Plains.* His unit was ordinarily based at Fort Laramie or Fort Leavenworth. First published in 1906, this early West memoir soon achieved fame and has been re-issued periodically. As late as 1996 the University of Oklahoma Press published a paperback edition of P.G. Lowe's classic. The reader learns that Lowe's company of dragoons set out for Fort St. Vrain from Fort Laramie in the spring of 1858. They were ordered to aid Major Sedgwick and Colonel Edwin Sumner on their punitive campaign against the Cheyenne. Flood water of the South Platte prevented Lowe's company from meeting Sedgwick at Fort St. Vrain. However, Sedgwick moved out and eventually met up with the Dragoons northeast of St. Vrain's. Sedgwick and Sumner's presence that summer of 1858 shows that Fort St. Vrain was occasionally co-opted by the military during campaigns against the Indians.

Shortly thereafter, Lowe resigned his commission and went into a freight-hauling and outfitting business with two partners. Their route was eastern Kansas to Denver, and when they could obtain government contracts, this business was highly lucrative. The mining industry around Denver was also creating good opportunities. When Lowe arrived in Denver late July or early August, 1859 he and his partners set up shop. Then, Lowe says, "I set the [mule] train crew to putting up hay, which paid very well" (Lowe 279). His participation in the St. Vrain Claim Club was intended to protect his access to the rich hay along the South Platte north of Denver. That the Claim Club members took these claims seriously is indicated by an incident recorded in the *St. Vrain Record Book.* The members took action against a Mr. Hawken who was "squatting" on Graham's claim and "to the great harm" of the latter. Hawken seems to have settled himself right in downtown St. Vrain township on lots owned by Graham.

Hawken and his companion were given one day to remove themselves from the area, and this they did without further protest. From a modern perspective, this anecdote may place the wretched Hawken in a pitiable light. For it is likely that he was merely putting up hay as he had done in the past from lands along the South Platte which had never before been claimed as privately owned. Well, now they were privately owned and the new "owners" meant to enforce their claims with their fists and rifles if need be. No wonder P.G. Lowe, who rarely saw Fort St. Vrain himself, was anxious to have his name on the official list.

One last point. Byers' newspaper noted in June, 1859 that "local farm produce from the 'bottom lands' along Boulder, St. Vrain (Creeks) and the South Platte river were found to be on sale in Denver markets" (reported in Shwayder, I: 13). Byers' vision of the area was consistently tied to his "boosterism" on behalf of agriculture—and the St. Vrain Claim Club was of the type, an Agricultural Claim Club as opposed to the urban folks' "People's Courts" and the prospectors' "Miner's Courts." Byers and Co. had a tripartite vision of industry in their Jefferson Territory: mining, agriculture—and tourism. This had become rather a traditional view since the assessments of Fremont and Gilpin had been published. But Byers, as usual, put his money into these enterprises, including a claim at Hot Sulphur Springs where the mineral waters and healthy mountain air were perfect for all comers to these "Swiss Alps of the American West" who needed the services of a health spa environment—often and especially for sufferers of tuberculosis.

The 1859 settlers quickly moved forward to create basic infrastructures—irrigation ditch companies, roads, bridges, mail and freight-hauling services. Every settler had to become his or her own surveyor, measuring off fields by tieing a strip of colored cloth to a wagon wheel and counting the rotations. On December 7, 1859 Fort St. Vrain procured a toll road charter from the Jefferson Territorial government to permit the Colorado Wagon Road Company to connect St. Vrain to Golden City. C.P. Hall of Fort Lupton was elected to represent the district at the Jefferson Territorial assembly. The St. Vrain Ditch Company petitioned the county government for a charter to build an irrigation canal off St. Vrain Creek. At some point, a bridge across the South Platte river was built. This seems to be the same toll bridge called the "Boughton Bridge" after an early settler

Martin Van Buren Boughton was at Fort St. Vrain for a time and then acquired a ranching operation farther east and downstream along the South Platte. An early settler, David Hodgson, recalled:

> A man by the name of Harrison and his wife and I came by the Platte River Road as we wanted to take in Boulder City. We arrived at Ft. St. Vrain on the 28th or 29th of May, 1861. I remember well we drove between the gate of the Fort and a house, [and] this

"A toll bridge was built in the early 1860's crossing the South Platter River near Old Fort St. Vrain. This is probably the Boughton Bridge which David Hodgson paid one dollar to cross. It led to Golden." Photo from Archives, Colorado Historical Society, used with permission.

129

house was about twenty feet from the gate on the south. The gate to the Fort was at the south east corner of the Fort. There was man by the name of Martin Boughton and his brother Ed, at the Fort at this time, who owed and kept a Toll Bridge across the Platte River about three fourths of a mile south west of the Fort. Harrison and I each paid one dollar Toll and drove over the bridge. Boughton was living at the Fort at that time taking care of the property in the absence of the proprietor who was away in St.Louis (Platteville Herald, Feb. 12, 1915, "Reminiscences").

Thus the beginnings of government were launched at Old Fort St. Vrain. Very early in the planning for a Jefferson Territory, Nebraska politicians lobbied for post offices in "the Pikes Peak Gold Region." On January 18, 1859, the Nebraska Territorial authorities designated Fort Lupton and Fort St. Vrain as post offices. Old Fort St. Vrain, then, was one of the two first post offices in what became two years hence, Weld County. Hiram J. Graham was the first postmaster. The fact that Fort St. Vrain had a postal stamp and a postmaster does not entail, however, that there would be mail delivery. During the summer of 1859, The *Rocky Mountain News* editorials complained that the nearest source of mail was Fort Laramie, 250 miles north.

Sometime between 1860 and 1861, Graham's successor, Andrew Lumry built a cottonwood log cabin to be used as post office and courthouse of St. Vrain County, soon-to-be Weld County (February, 1861). There the deeds were recorded, commissioners met, and authoritative documents filed. Stage coaches stopped, mail was dropped off and picked up. Judges had been appointed, and court was held. The *St. Vrain Record Book* cites the occasion of a marriage and, early in 1863, the first Grand Jury Session in Weld County was held in the log courthouse.

The stage line that passed from Denver to Fort Laramie on the "Mountain Run" from Denver to Salt Lake City, used the South Platte adobe forts as stations between 1862 and

1864 when the Sioux along the Oregon Trail (they'd been in a warlike mood since the Grattan debacle) made life more than usually dangerous and Ben Holladay, owner of the Overland Stage Co., had to route his coaches along the South Platte. He disliked doing this because it was inefficient and passengers suffered greater hardships. In those years, Fort St. Vrain was either a "swing station" where horse teams were changed and passengers could stretch their legs, or a "home station," where passengers were put up for the night. The earliest settlers in the area recall the log cabin "courthouse" also being a "hotel" where men slept on the floor, five or six tucked side by side.

The question of Fort St. Vrain's usefulness as a stage station has turned out to be one of the most difficult in this entire study to pin down. Books about the Overland Stage Co. yield almost no information. I have concluded, then, that it was a mail drop-off place to serve area settlers, and perhaps

Sometime between 1860 and 1863 a log structure was built to house the St. Vrain County Records. It was moved to pioneer David Birkle's farm near Platteville and then to the site of Fort Vasquez. It now resides in Greeley's Historic District, Centennial Village. Thus, one of Colorado's first courthouses still exists.

pick up produce bound for market in Denver, but that the stage company made limited use of it after 1863, even as a swing station. Holladay's company created a station two miles downstream at "the great bend of the South Platte," called "Big Bend Station." Today, there is a farmhouse there and in its yard a simple sign along SH 60 near Milliken, Colorado,. But, besides a vague awareness that it had been a stop for the Overland Stage, details of the use the company made of Big Bend Station are lacking. As long as the stage stopped at Big Bend Station, it would by-pass Fort St. Vrain and proceed to Fort Vasquez, 12 miles upstream and about the right distance for the next stop. Local traditions also hold that Fort Vasquez was a "post office," and probably mail was handled there. It did not have an official cancellation stamp, however, and its use by the stage company was determined by two criteria: convenience and amenities, especially food. Or, horse handlers. Whether a stop was convenient and attractive depended on the neighboring settlers. Which ones were able to keep horseflesh in good shape and have them ready for duty at the swing stations? Which ones were prepared to turn their kitchens into bakeries and dining halls, their haylofts into hotels? Above all, which ones could do all of this? The Paul family at Fort Vasquez probably had a sweeter hayloft, a better cook or wrangler among its membership than the Lumry's at Fort St. Vrain.

As soon as the Indian problem had been "solved" by shoving these "wild men" onto reservations, Holladay refined his routes, sending his stagecoaches from Latham to Greeley, from there to LaPorte and on to Virginia Dale and Laramie over the highway now known as U.S. 287. It is clear why he favored Latham Station, clear because a rare and fascinating diary by the lady of the house, Ella Bailey, records what it meant to serve hospitality on the Overland Stage Line. "Baked 51 pies. Tired as a begger . . . Baked twenty-three pies and three thousand cookies and ginger snaps (Mar. 3, 1869)[5]. In 1868 the county seat of Weld was moved from Fort St. Vrain to Latham, and although the historians tell us "the circumstances behind the move are vague," this writer believes that Ella Bailey's pies played a part in the county commissioners' decision.

The move also seems to be related to the re-establishment of stagecoach lines about 1865 and the preferences of Ben Holladay in the mid-1860's for the Platte river and Cache La Poudre routes to the north of Fort St. Vrain.. At this time, then, the north-south axis from Greeley to Denver became a subsidiary route. Only when Indian uprisings threatened the east-west routes did the stagecoach lines re-route to include Denver and its station to the north, Fort St. Vrain. Nevertheless, Fort St. Vrain remained a stagecoach stop for local stage lines, while not being a noted "swing station" for as long as the stagecoach lines provided transportation until they were replaced by railroad routes.

Notes to Chapter Six
The St. Vrain Claim Club

[1]Cleon Roberts, *Fort Lupton History 1836 to 1976,* Fort Lupton, Colorado Centennial-Bicentennial Committee of Fort Lupton, 1976, 96.

[2]This information synthesized from Robert Perkin, *The Rocky Mountain News: The First One Hundred Years,* Garden City, New York; Doubleday & Co., 1959, 135–139.

[3]From *Pikes Peak Gold Rush Guidebooks of 1859: Tierney, Parson and Others,* LeRoy Hafen, ed., *Southwest Historical Series* IX, 222–224.

[4]Perkin 229.

[5]Ella Bailey's fascinating diary is available at the Greeley Municipal Museum, Greeley, CO and in an edited version by Agnes Wright Spring, Colorado State Historian, Stephen Hart library, CHS, Denver, CO.

The daughter of Marcellin St. Vrain, Mary Louise Sopris, and the DAR regent perform the unveiling ceremony.

VII. Dedication

ort St. Vrain's adobe bricks had eroded away, been trampled by cattle, been picked up as souvenirs, been used for other edifices by local pioneers. Fort St. Vrain's walls fell into partial decay. The early traders' visions of great steamship docks along the South Platte had long ago faded. The South Platte was deemed "a mile wide and an inch deep: too thick to drink, too thin to plow." By 1875, the mail was delivered to Platteville (founded with the railroad in 1871) and one of the last functions of the old fort disappeared. The Union Pacific railroad connecting Denver to Cheyenne passed about four miles east of Old Fort St. Vrain. For practical purposes, the old fort was now deemed useless, and a silent tug-of-war developed between those who thought its memory and history worth preserving, and those who were resigned to considering its obsolescence a rationale for forgetting it altogether.

Yet, for local people it never lost its fascination. As a reminder that its 4th of July tradition went as far back as Fremont's expedition, the early settlers would make a picnic spot of the old fort—or—out of respect for the private ownership of the land—picnicked on Wildcat Mound across the river. Since, by early July the river was almost always quite shallow, especially for picnickers on horseback, a hunt for arrowheads or other treasures at Old Fort St. Vrain added adventure to the day. Thus, in 1871, Orpha NcNitt, a frontier bride of Civil War veteran and surveyor Alpheus McNitt, wrote "back east to the States," to her Wisconsin family about her first Independence Day with her new husband in this land which had been Colorado Territory for only ten

years. On July 12, 1871, Orpha described a day at Wildcat
Mound and the old fort:

> Along the bluff [on Wildcat, west of the river] the
> wind and rain have hollowed out places almost like
> caves. A roof can extend ten feet or more making a fine
> shelter. Many people have carved their names into the
> soft rock walls. The most interesting are names of sol-
> diers with the dates 1842 and 1843. I suppose they
> were with exploration parties for our government.
>
> While we were resting after dinner, the men told
> us about something we had seen from the top of the
> bluff. They said it is the ruin of Ft. St. Vrain. It was
> built in 1838 by the Bent brothers and Col. Ceran St.
> Vrain as a trading post and later became a halfway
> station between Ft. Laramie in Wyoming and Ft. Bent
> a long way to the south of us.
>
> Alpheus explained that our Fourth of July picnic is
> keeping up a tradition begun by Gen. Fremont when he
> was making his first journey of exploration into the
> northwest. He reached Ft. St. Vrain on July 3, 1843. The
> next day he raised the United States flag over the fort
> and declared a holiday. This was the first celebration of
> Independence Day in what is now Colorado Territory.

The McNitts and one or two other couples crossed the
South Platte, carefully avoiding quicksand. They explored the
fort, noting, as had Francis Parkman twenty-five years before,
a dilapidated condition. Orpha reports that they found a few
arrowheads around the walls, and tells her family, ". . . we
could see that the fort was divided into rooms for the traders
and their visitors. Some of the traders married squaws and
lived in the fort. I had heard of an old well where a canon [sic]
had been dumped, but I couldn't find it (McNitt 49–50).

Eighty years later, such rumors still persisted. Colorado's
prolific and famous state historian, LeRoy Hafen, made a public appeal to the landowners of Old Fort St. Vrain to delay a
proposed land leveling operation. Historic preservation issues

do not often make front page headlines, but on July 25, 1952 the *Rocky Mountain News* announced: "Dispute is Raging Over Leveling of Old Fort Site Near Denver." The DAR of Greeley had obtained promises from the landowner to "beautify the site, put in a road and make it accessible to the public." The story called Old Fort St. Vrain a "bastion of the fur trade days," and 'the scene in 1843 of Colorado's first 'ice cream social.'" LeRoy Hafen told the *News* that "one reason he opposed disturbing the old fort scene is to give additional time for checking two old rumors of a mysterious tunnel and a buried brass cannon."

One person who visited fort St. Vrain in the early days later wrote an escape tunnel was dug deep under the earth from inside the fort to the banks of the Platte," he said. "The tunnel was to have been used in case the fort ever was overwhelmed by a superior Indian force. . . .

Another visitor to the fort reported that an old brass cannon was tossed into the fort well to hide it during an Indian attack (*Rocky Mountain News*).

The article concluded by summarizing Fremont's two stopovers at Fort St. Vrain, noting , "It was on the second trip Colorado saw its first ice cream party, Dr. Hafen said. William Gilpin, later to become the first territorial governor, was a member of the expedition and recorded later that snow was brought from the mountains for homemade ice cream with which to celebrate the Fourth of July in 1843."

September 16, 1952, when Dr. Hafen did search for the cannon in the well, he brought a Colorado School of Mines geophysics student and two WWII metal detectors. Although there was not time to cover all of the near-acre site, two signals alerted the state historian and his helper of the presence of metals below the surface. Shallow digging revealed no evidence of a tunnel, or a cannon, or any other metallic substance. The search would have to be postponed. The next day's *News* reported "Indian Legend Remains a Mystery." After a brief historical background on Fort St. Vrain, "One of Area's First," the reporter quoted Hafen as saying that "Chief Friday's story of the massacre and the cannon was retold at monument dedication ceremonies in 1911 by Marshall Cook, an 1858-er in Northern Colorado." Marshall Cook died in 1884, however, and his story must have been retold by a surrogate storyteller in 1911.

Because some people thought its memory worth preserving, Old Fort St. Vrain has attracted these attentions and more since 1868 when the county seat of Old Weld was moved to Latham near Greeley. Active support came from the Greeley Centennial Chapter of the DAR in 1910 and 1911 and from Public Service Company of Colorado and the Colorado Historical Society in the 1960's. The earliest efforts, however, apparently were launched by the Denver, Laramie and Northwestern railroad, in 1909, as outlined in *The Sunday News-Times*, Denver, Colo., October 24, 1909. The plans were as follows:

PRESERVE OLD TRADING POSTS: D.L. & N. RESTORING ST. VRAIN

FORMER FORT TO BE ATTRACTION AT NEW TOWN; STILL IN FAIR CONDITION

COL. R.A. EATON'S PLEA FOR MAKING HISTORIC PLACES KNOWN TO TOURISTS

These plans came to naught. A year passed. At its annual planning meeting January, 1910, the Greeley Centennial Chapter of the Daughters of the American Revolution records in a small, leather-bound book the interest the chapter had begun to take in the old trails and forts of the area. Experts presented informational programs, and the DAR decided to sponsor a project which would leave a large granite marker at the site of Old Fort St. Vrain. A year later, in mid-June, the impressive stone, etched with a legend, was dedicated. The ceremony had at first been planned for Flag Day, June 14th but was postponed a week. Early in 1912, the DAR historian summarized from the previous year's minutes:

June 22nd was a proud day for our Chapter when a large number of the members and their friends gathered at the site of Old Fort St. Vrain to dedicate the Monument, erected by the Centennial State Chapter and the friends who so generously assisted them. Many pioneers who remembered those stirring times were present from the surrounding country. . . . [Though] this depleted our treasury, we are proud of the results and here extend thanks to all who so generously assisted us in any way. . . . [And] it is interesting to note Mrs. [Mary St. Vrain] Sopris, daughter of Marcellus St. Vrain and niece of Col. Ceran St. Vrain was present. She was born in this fort. Her daughter, Mrs. Wiggenhorn of Salt Lake and her son Albert Sopris were also present. Their pictures are placed in the Post Card Album (Minutes of the Greeley Centennial Chapter, DAR).

Major Denver and regional newspapers gave good coverage both before and after the event, often with pictorial additions, especially because so many prominent pioneers were present at the dedication and the picnic afterward. Although Marshall Cook could not have been there, many who well remembered the Indian War of 1864 and the appalling climax at Sand Creek were there to reminisce. Territorial status was achieved, Civil War raged to the east—stirring times, indeed. Fort St. Vrain, because it was there and had always been ON THE MAP, had set a precedent for northeastern Colorado settlers. The *Denver Post* called it "Ancient Fort St. Vrain." (June 1, 1911). The monument was listed with other historically significant sites in the National Register of the DAR.

Some samples from area newspaper coverage appear as follows:

NIECE OF THE FOUNDER OF HISTORIC STRUCTURE ATTENDS IMPRESSIVE CEREMONIES
[Special to the News]

Greeley, Colo., June 22—With a niece of Colonel Ceran St.

Vrain on one side and Mrs. B.D. Sanborn, regent of the local chapter D.A.R. on the other, the monument marking the site of old Fort St. Vrain, twenty miles south of here, was unveiled at noon today. The niece of the famous explorer is Mrs. Mary Sopris of Denver, widow of General Sopris. Her daughter, Mrs. J.B. Wiggenhorn, and her son, Albert, were present. Her father was Marcellus St. Vrain, a brother of Ceran.

The unveiling came at the close of an interesting program, which included singing of patriotic songs, reminiscences by pioneers and a history of the work of the D.A.R. by Mrs. E.B. Thayer, state vice-regent. More than 300 persons witnessed the ceremony, including officers of the local chapter and a large number of Greeley business men.

Mrs. Sopris was born at the fort, in 1842 [sic], but her parents left there when she was one year old. Asked to make a speech, she said:

"I am glad to be here today and glad that a monument has been erected to mark this site. I want to thank the ladies who are responsible for it."

Judge Jacobs recalls the early history of Colorado at Old Fort St. Vrain, June 22, 1911.

Other prominent pioneers who spoke were Judge W.S. Hammitt of Platteville, M.H. Coffin of Longmont, C.W. Burbridge and R.W. Piper.

The four corners of the fort were marked with stones and flags. The new state flag was hung below Old Glory, the two being run up during the unveiling and while the crowd was singing "America."

The monument, which is five feet high and four feet across the base, and which is made of Salida granite, bears [an] inscription. . . .

Judge John T. Jacobs delivered the address of the day, paying high tribute to the founder of the fort and the pioneers of the West. While he was speaking scores of children were gathering beads and arrow heads within sound of his voice.

Rocky Mountain News, June 22, 1911

On June 23, 1911, The *Denver Republican* carried a story about the dedication on its first inside page:

OLD FORT ST. VRAIN MARKED BY MASSIVE GRANITE MONUMENT
Patriotic Society places enduring Memorial on the spot where some interesting Colorado history was made

GREELEY Colo—June 22—(Special)—Amid the crumbling walls of Old Fort St. Vrain a monument of granite was placed today under the auspices of Centennial State Chapter, D.A.R., to mark the spot about which clusters some of the most thrilling early history of Weld county.

There 300 people gathered today and with appropriate ceremonies unveiled the granite marker, which is six feet high, four feet wide, two feet six inches thick and bears [an] inscription. . . .

The granite markers at the four corners of the fort were the gift of Capt. Thomas G. Macy, a pioneer of Greeley.

The program began with an invocation by the Rev. T.C. Brockway, who recited "The Recessional." The audience joined in singing "The Star-Spangled Banner," and Judge John T. Jacobs followed with an address concerning the early history of the fort. Mrs. E.B. Thayer of Greeley, state vice regent of the D.A.R., told of the work and aims of the order in tracing and marking battlefield[s] and other historic spots.

One of the most interesting features of the occasion was the introduction of Mrs. Mary Sopris, wife of Gen. Sopris, and a niece of Col. St. Vrain, who was born in the old fort in 1848 [sic]. She was accompanied by her son [sic: grandson] Albert Sopris, and her daughter, Mrs. J.B. Wiggenhorn of Salt Lake. Mrs. Sopris said she remembered little of the early history of the fort, having removed to New Mexico when a young child. She is a daughter of Marcellus St. Vrain.

Then the monument's drapery, a large American flag, was lifted by Mrs. B.D. Sanborn, regent of Centennial chapter, and Mrs. Sopris, as the audience sang, "Columbia."

Many of the oldest pioneers of Weld county were present, among them M.H. Coffin of Longmont, who remembered St. Vrain well when the latter conducted a trading store in Denver in the early sixties. Judge W.S. Hammitt, G.W. Burbridge, Perkin, Hudson and other from the Platteville country gave reminiscences.

The pioneers remained after the exercises, had a picnic dinner and indulged in reminiscences.

Probably no one person did more to bring about the erection of a monument on the site of old Fort St. Vrain than Judge John T. Jacobs of Greeley, of the local chapter of the Sons of the American Revolution. Over a year ago he became interested in searching for the sites of all old forts of Weld county. He discovered old books recounting the history of St. Vrain and other pioneers and studied well known histories and books on explorations. He brought the matter to the attention of the local chapter of the D.A.R. last February and the monument was planned.

Today Judge Jacobs in delivering his patriotic address at the unveiling of the monument recounted the early and romantic history associated with Fort St. Vrain. He recalled that Lieut. Long was the first white man to visit the St. Vrain locality 96 years ago. It was a wilderness even when St. Vrain established his trading post with the Indians, building the fort principally for that purpose. In 1837 there was not a dwelling of the white man nearer than Fort Laramie, Wyo., or Fort Bent on the Arkansas [sic]. He told of the coming of Gen. Fremont to the fort in 1842 while on his famous exploration trip, he and Col. Ceran St. Vrain being friends. Francis Parkman stopped at the fort in 1846 and tells of his visit in his "Oregon Trail."

Judge Jacobs then pictured the coming of the first settlers to the valley of the St. Vrain, the protection the fort gave them from Indians, the splendid courage of the early settlers, their faithfulness, patriotism, hardships and success, and said:

"This stone today is not only a monument to the gallant Col. Ceran St. Vrain, the band of explorers, the historians, but also to those noble patriots, the pioneers of the St. Vrain." He concluded by paying a tribute to the local chapter of the Daughters of the American Revolution for their patriotism in marking the site of the old fort.

According to some traditional wisdom, one primary source of historical information was Marshall Cook's manuscript, "Early History of Colorado," of which portions were read at the dedication ceremony. The variations in reporting Mary Louise St. Vrain Sopris' birthdate has given rise to a great deal of confusion about when Marcellin St. Vrain left the fort for the last time; I feel confident however, in putting forth a day in the late spring or early summer of 1846, as stated in a preceding chapter. One last note about these newspaper coverages: the credit given to Ceran St. Vrain for his role in the existence of the trading post is based on a misunderstanding, apparently, of the central role played by Marcellin in managing the post and of the Bent brothers, William and George, in seeing to its construction. Ceran St. Vrain was certainly a source of funds for the building, as he was a senior partner in the Bent, St. Vrain Co. There is very little evidence, however, to show that he spent actual time at Fort St. Vrain, and the only safe assumption to make is that he probably used it as a rest house on journeys to Fort Laramie, if and when he had occasion to venture that far north.

A few years prior to the dedication of the monument, Francis W. Cragin was exercising another kind of "dedication" to historical preservation, interviewing Weld County's old-timers and taking pictures of the ruins of Fort Vasquez and Fort St. Vrain. His collection, now at the Colorado Springs Pioneer Museum, constitutes a remarkable effort in preserving Colorado's early history. An appreciative LeRoy Hafen, in his article "Fort St. Vrain" quotes Cragin's notebooks extensively, noting that it was Cragin who carefully measured the dimensions of Fort St. Vrain, so that we know precisely that it was 106' × 127'.

In 1943, the ranch land around the monument, excepting that reserved to private ownership, was sold, and Public Service Company of Colorado put up a substation and residence, duly recording the new use on a warranty deed filed with Weld County. Nine years later, on September 23, 1952, the land around the fort, approximately one acre, was conveyed to Weld County for "ten dollars and other valuable considerations." The warranty deed included right-of-way via a 30-foot-wide road leading to the granite marker, napped as "Monument Road" off Weld County Road 40. The site is described:

> A rectangular parcel of land 106' wide and 127' long, marked at the corners with concrete blocks, being the site of old "Fort St. Vrain", as shown on the plat of the Town of Fort St. Vrain (now vacated), and being on a parcel of land shown on said plat bordered on the North by Roubidoux Avenue, on the East by Ceran Place, on the South by Sarpey Avenue and on the West by Kiowa Street, and, at the approximate center of which is situate "Fort St. Vrain Monument", erected in the year 1911 by the Centennial State Chapter, Daughters of the American Revolution, and being located in the Southeast Quarter (SE 1/4) of Section twenty-six (26) Township Four (4) North, Range Sixty-seven (67) West of the 6th P.M.; the plan of Fort St. Vrain being on file in the Office of the County Clerk and Recorder of Weld County,

Colorado. . . . Together with a right of way for a public road. . . .

On September 29th following, the Weld County Commissioners issued a formal acceptance of the parcel and "dedicated the same to the public."

Fifty years later, the Colorado Historical Society in partnership with Otero Junior College and Public Service Company of Colorado reminded the public of the fort's existence by launching an archaeological excavation at Old Fort St. Vrain. Historians have not contested Guy L. Peterson's conclusion in a monograph summary of his C.S.U. Masters' thesis: ". . . the fort had lost . . . much of its archaeological value in 1951 [for] . . . the owner leveled what remained of its walls. . . ." Peterson summarizes the archaeology of the site from 1967, when lead archaeologist, Galen Baker, was on the faculty of Otero.

Three miles to the south, Public Service Company had, by 1969, built a nuclear energy generating plant and named it after the old fort. In an effort to clarify the early commercial nature of the fur-trading post, PSC helped fund historical research through the Colorado Historical Society. In a facsimile museum at the site of the power plant, three miles southeast of the old fort, results of the excavation and summaries of what was known about old Fort St. Vrain were available in well illustrated pamphlets and brochures. The museum at the new fort St. Vrain is now used as a company training center. PSC donated its display cases, many artifacts, pictures and printed materials to the Platteville Pioneer Museum and the Platteville Historical Society.

The archaeological research was less rewarding. The aim of it was to discover artifacts which would reveal the lifestyle and the nature of the inhabitants of the fort. These were the sort of treasures sought, not buried bricks of gold. There had long been rumors of a cemetery outside the north walls. This was not ascertained. Inside the perimeters, a back hoe was used to create a trench five feet deep, but the researchers, according to Guy L. Peterson, found only some ceramic and

During the 1980's the site of Old Fort St. Vrain was used as a trash dump. Photo courtesy Longmont Times-Call, Sept. 24, 1985.

leather pieces, 47 beads, 17 samples of adobe, some animal bones, a few evidences of charcoal, gypsum, concrete, and "manufactured objects" which were probably imported to the site long after the trading post closed around 1846. Local newspapers headlined the dig as yielding "slim pickings."

Although the archaeological evidence disappointed expectations, Fort St. Vrain continues to hold a place in local memory. Its story was again told in the Centennial edition of the *Greeley Tribune,* April 3, 1970, because it was the beginnings and center of settlement and government in Weld County. The article reflected nostalgically that the proposed town of St. Vrain had "blocks numbered up to 420."

Finally, when the Weld County Historical Society was formed in 1984, one of its co-founders, Carol Rein Shwayder, remarked: "Of the 17 County Seats named that day [September 9, 1861, at the first Colorado Territorial Legislative meeting],—6 are now ghost towns—including Weld's own St.

Vrain—which is marked only by a granite marker—in a corn-field—the site used as TRASH DUMP!—Is this any way to treat our first County Seat?" The Weld Historical Society's attempt to work with the county commissioners to create a park at the one-acre site came to naught. The newspaper which reported the old historic site's modern status as a trash dump was not even located in Weld County but rather, in Boulder County, the Times-Call of Longmont, Colorado. Ironically, Old Fort St. Vrain was once again in a kind of no-man's land, owned by Weld County (which has never been in a position to build and maintain parks) but even as public property, recognized by very few individuals. The access road, Weld County Road 40, was an exercise in misdirection, difficult to find, a gravel one-way track marked halfway to the site with a caution sign: "Not a through road." Many persons, even local people familiar with the general lay of the land, thought the access road a private driveway and turned back before reaching the site.

Eventually, in 2001, the Weld County deeded the site (which had not been marked and was hard to find) to the Platteville Historical Society and agreed to fence the marker and reset the corner markers where the fort once stood. The sign "Monument Road" was to be placed along U.S. Highway 85 at the intersection of County Road 40. About the same time, the Colorado Historical Society included Old Fort St. Vrain in its official list of commemorative sites. Thus, preservation efforts by local Weld citizens, Bonnie Smith of the D.A.R. and the D.A.R. Centennial Chapter in Greeley, Ruth Gartrell, Sally Miller, and members of the Platteville Historical Society, Weld County preservationist Carol Shwayder, the Weld County attorney and other county officials among the Commissioners, and this researcher, working together, at long last brought Old Fort St. Vrain into the light where its pristine setting can be enjoyed and its story heard.

Those who persevere are rewarded. Facing west, they see the South Platte, sparkling in patches reflected by the sun, partially hidden by trees. They stand on a modest bluff above the river just as trappers almost two hundred years ago stood by the walls of the old fort—the sublime and whitened peaks of Long and Meeker over-shadowing the blue-violet foothills below the Never Summer Range. Perhaps they know from what they have heard about the trapper, trader, Indian, Unionist, colonizer, businessman and preservationists who have stood here to honor their past that only in their awareness of their past they are fully themselves.

Selected Works Consulted

Anderson, George L. "The Middle Park Claims Club" *Colorado Magazine.* 16: (Nov., 1939) 189–193.

_____. "The El Paso Claims Club, 1859-1862." *Colorado Magazine.* 13: (March, 1936). 41-53.

Bauer, William H., Ozment, James L. and Willard, John H. *Colorado Postal History: The Post Offices.* J-B Publishing Co.: The Crete News, Inc., no loc., 1971.

Blassingame, Wyatt. Bent's Fort: *Crossroads of the Great West.* Garrard Publishing Company: Champagne, Illinois, 1967.

Broadhead, Edward. *Ceran St. Vrain, 1802-1870.* Pueblo, Colorado: Pueblo County Historical Society, 1990 [1982].

Brown, Seletha. *Rivalry At The River . . . In Colorado's Fur Forts.* Johnson Publishing Company: Boulder, Colorado, 1972 rept. [1959].

Cain, Suzanne, Marlatt, Alberta, et.al. [The Longmont Writer's Club]. *The St. Vrain Valley: Peek into the Past.* St. Vrain Valley School District RE-1J, Longmont, CO 1975.

Carter, Harvey L. "Marcellin St. Vrain" in *The Mountain Men and the Fur Trade of the Far West.* LeRoy R. Hafen, editor. Arthur H. Clark Company: Glendale, CA, 1966. Vol 3: 273-277.

Coel, Margaret. *Chief Left Hand: Southern Arapaho.* Norman: Oklahoma UP, 1981.

Conrad, Howard Louis. *Uncle Dick Wootton: Pioneer Frontiersman of the Rocky Mountain Region.* Lincoln: Nebraska UP, 1980 [1957].

Cook, Marshall. *Early History of Colorado.* Unpublished ms. Denver, CO: Colorado Historical Society. ca. 1880's.

Dunham, Harold H.. "Ceran St. Vrain." In *The Mountain Men and the Fur Trade of the Far West.* LeRoy R. Hafen, ed. Arthur H. Clark Company: Glendale, CA, 1966. Vol. 5:297-316.

Fremont, John Charles. *Memoirs of My Life.* New York: Belford, Clark & Co. Ca. 1896.

Garrard, Lewis H. *Wah-to-Yah and the Taos Trail.* Norman: Oklahoma UP, 1955.

Gates, Zethyl. "Fremont's Hitchhiker." Unpublished ms. Loveland, CO, 2000.

Geffs, Mary L. *Under Ten Flags: A History of Weld County,* Colorado. Greeley, Colorado, 1938.

Gilbert, Bil. *The Life of Joseph Walker, Master of the Frontier.* New York: Athenaeum, 1983.

Goode, W.H. *Outposts of Zion.* Cincinnati: Hitchcock and Poe, 1864.

Gowan, Fred. *Rocky Mountain Rendezvous.* 3rd printing. Provo: Brightam Young UP, 1978.

Grinnel, George Bird. *The Cheyenne Indians,* I. Lincoln & London: University of Nebraska Press, 1973 ([Yale UP, 1923].

Hafen, LeRoy R. *Broken Hand: The Life of Tomas Fitzpatrick, Mountain Man, Guide and Indian Agent.* Lincoln & London: Nebraska UP, 1981 [1931].

____. "Fort St. Vrain," in *The Colorado Magazine.* Denver, Colorado: The State Historical Society of Colorado, Publisher. October, 1952: Vol 29, No. 4: 241-255.

____, ed. The Mountain Men and the Fur Trade of the Far West. "Bibliography and Index." Arthur H. Clark Company: Glendale, CA, 1954-1968. Vol. 10: 144.

____, ed. *Pikes Peck Guide Books: Tierney, Parsons & Others.* Southwest Historical Series IX. Philadelphia: Porcupine Press, 1974.

Hodgson, David. "Reminiscences." *Platteville Herald* (Feb. 12) 1915. See also *Coloardo Magazine.*

Hyde, George E. *Life of George Bent.* Savoie Lottinville, ed. Norman: Oklahoma UP, 1968.

Johnston, Ralph E. *Old Tangle Eye.* Boston: Houghton-Mifflin Co., 1954.

Judge, W. James. "The Archaeology of Ft. Vasquez" in *Four Forts Along the Platte: Auto Tour of Fort Lupton, Fort Jackson, Fort Vasquez, and Fort St. Vrain.* May, 1997. Rpt. Orig. in *The Colorado Magazine.* The Colorado Historical Society: Denver, CO.. Vol 48, No. 3 (Summer) 1971: 181–203.

Krakel, Dean F. *South Platte Country: A History of Old Weld County, Colorado, 1739–1900.* The Powder River Publishers: Laramie, WY., 1954.

Lavender, David. *Bent's Fort.* Lincoln: University of Nebraska Press, 1952.

Leyendecker, Liston, ed. *Hiram Pitt Bennet: Pioneer, Frontier Lawyer, Politician.* Denver, Colorado: Colorado Historical Society, Monograph 2, 1988.

Lowe, Percival G. *Five Years a Dragoon ('49 to '54).* Norman: Oklahoma, UP, 1965 [1906].

Magoffin, Susan Shelby. *Down the Santa Fe Trail and into Mexico: The Diary of Susan Shelby Magoffin, 1846-1847.* Edited by Stella M. Drumm. Lincoln & London, Nebraska UP, 1982 [1926].

McNitt, Orpha Baldwin. *Letters from a Frontier Bride.* Edited and self-published by Emma Alice Hamm, Longmont, Colorado, 1993.

150

Office of Indian Affairs. Records of the Upper Platte and Arkansas Indian Agency. Denver, CO: National Archives, Rocky Mountain Region. Microfilm # 889.

Perkin, Robert L. The Rocky Mountain News: *The First One Hundred Years.* Garden City, New York: Doubleday & Co., 1959.

Peterson, Guy L. *Four Forts of the South Platte.* Monograph rpt., 1982. Orig. in Periodical-Journal of the Council on America's Military Past, Vol 11, No.4, whole no. 45. 1982.

Propst, Nell Brown. *Forgotten People.* Boulder, CO: Pruett Publishing Co., 1979.

Quaife, Milo Milton, ed. *Kit Carson's Autobiography.* Lincoln: Nebraska UP, 1966 [1935].

Roberts, Cleon. *Fort Lupton, Colorado: The First Hundred and Forty Years.* Colorado Centennial-Bicentennial Committee of Fort Lupton, 1976.

Robertson, H.G. *Competitive Struggle.* Boise, ID: Tamarack Press, 1998

Sage, Rufus. *Rocky Mountain Life.* Rpt. 1857 ed. Lincoln: University of Nebraska Press, 1982 [1846].

Shwayder, Carol Rein, ed. *Weld County—Old and New: I.* Unicorn Press, 1983.

_____. *Weld County Old and New, V:* "People and Places, Historical Gazetteer, Dictionary of Place Names Prehistoric Indians to 1992." Greeley,Colorado: Unicorn Ventures, 1992.

Sopris, W.R. "My Grandmother, Mrs. Marcellin St. Vrain." *Colorado Magazine.* (Mar. 1945). 63–68.

Spring, Agnes Wright, ed. *Ella Bailey's Diary. Denver Westerner's Brand Book,* Co. 1960.

Spring, Agnes Wright. "Rush to the Rockies." *Colorado Magazine.* 36:2 (April 1959). 95–129.

Stone, Wilbur Fisk, ed. *History of Colorado, I.* The S.J. Clarke Publishing Company: Chicago, Ill., 1918.

Talbot, Theodore. *The Journals of Theodore Talbot, 1843 and 1849–52.* Charles H. Carey, ed. Portland, Oregon: Metropolitan Press, 1931.

Trenholm,. Virginia Cole. *The Arapahoes, Our People.* Norman: Oklahoma UP, 1986 [1970].

Ubbelohde, Carl. *A Colorado History.* Boulder, CO: Pruett Press, 1965.

Wislizenus, F.A. *A Journey to the Rock Mountains in the Year 1839.* Fairfield, Washington: The Galleon Press, 1989.